Pineapple and Profits

WHY YOU'RE NOT YOUR BUSINESS

(AND WHY THAT MATTERS)

Kelly Townsend | Peter Frampton

Pineapple and Profits
Why you're not your business (and why that matters)

By Kelly Townsend and Peter Frampton

Publisher: Leaders Team LLC
Address: 5647 Naples Blvd, Naples, FL 34109
Website: leadersteam.com
Email: general@leadersteam.com

First Edition 2025
ISBN: 979-8-9931958-0-3

Table of contents

Introduction

Thank you for picking up this book.

That simple act tells us something important about you: You're ready for something different. You're tired of feeling controlled by your business instead of being the leader of it. You know there's a gap between where you are and where you want to be.

You're not alone. We have worked for decades with thousands of executives, thought leaders, and business owners who feel stuck and want to see more, do more, and get beyond what holds them back.

Our work with people like you, who have a commitment to grow themselves and grow their businesses, has shown us that our own growth comes from what we discover for ourselves. This book is intended to have you ignite something new for yourself. There's something about discovery that enlivens us, and some discoveries launch us into a new future. One such discovery came when Kelly met Peter. Peter's great charisma and talent for uniquely interpreting accounting broke through her personal barriers around finance and numbers. He's helped her, as well as thousands of others. Little did Kelly realize that their meeting would create an entirely new context for her business and her role as its owner.

What you'll discover

In this book, you'll learn to see your business as something separate from you—not to create distance, but to gain power.

You'll discover:

- How to identify and rebuild the limiting conversations and assumptions that constrain the growth of your business
- A simple framework that makes finance intuitive (you'll learn to RELAX!)
- Why you must think double when making every financial decision
- How to use your word to create your future value cycle

These aren't just concepts. They're tools that have transformed hundreds of businesses. They work because they transform how you see your operation, not just what you do.

But ... concepts and tools only work when you use them. So don't just read this book. Live it. Implement it. Make it real in your business. This is our invitation to you, and we're thrilled to be on the journey with you.

Your journey starts now

You picked up this book because something in your current approach isn't working. Maybe you know you're capable of more but can't see the path forward. Maybe you're simply ready to stop letting old stories run your future.

Whatever brought you here, know this: the business you want to build is possible. The freedom you seek is achievable. The impact you want to make is within reach.

Pineapple and Profits will challenge you to see the value of elevating your financial fluency and to reveal what becomes possible from the exercises in the book.

Let that future begin now.

Turn the page. Your new future is waiting.

Kelly Townsend and Peter Frampton

1

Pineapple

Imagine this: The buzz of a bustling market, the energy of a Saturday, the sweet, tangy smell of ripe pineapples filling the air. For Alicia, the owner of Alicia's Organic Market, each transaction feels electric, a personal triumph.

Now picture Carlos, who is there to buy a pineapple. Alicia is excited to sell it to her new customer. They exchange the pineapple for cash.

Now ask yourself: who sold the pineapple? It may seem obvious to you that Alicia sold the pineapple. Yet this is somewhat of a trick question. The answer is, Alicia didn't ... **the business** sold the pineapple.

Consider that every customer Alicia served from her organic business felt like a direct reflection of her effort—even her worth. Like most small business owners, this seemingly innocent experience plants a seed—a deeply rooted misconception that most small business owners and countless entrepreneurs stumble through and try to unlearn—the dangerous idea that *I am my business.* We will reveal shortly why this misconception can leave you and your business bounded and limited.

If you answered that Alicia sold the pineapple, you demonstrated something that affects most business owners: you collapsed the identity of an owner with the business itself. Trust us when we say: you are not alone. In workshops and our talks with small business owners, eight out of ten people give this same answer.

This collapse runs deeper than most realize. As people begin examining the internal conversations that reinforce this perspective, they discover just how thoroughly their sense of self has become entangled with their business identity.

Let's dive a bit deeper into the Carlos story. We saw how Carlos went to his local organic produce market to buy a pineapple from Alicia, who owns the fictional business, Alicia's Organic Market.

Who sold the pineapple?

Alicia
Owner

Carlos
Customer

At first glance, it appears that Alicia sold the pineapple to Carlos.

Did Alicia sell the pineapple?

Alicia
Owner

But actually, Alicia's *business* sold it. And that's a really critical point—through the lens of finance, the business entity sold the pineapple, not Alicia. She was fulfilling the role of owner as well as employee of the business. But financially, she did not enter into the transaction.

The business itself is selling the pineapple

Most small business owners believe that they *are their business*. But when you view situations from the point of view of what's best for the business versus what's best for you personally, situations show up for you differently.

You look to see what is in the best interests of your business, rather than what makes you personally comfortable (or uncomfortable). Demanding late fees or chasing rental payments from a tenant is not fun. But from the point of view of the business, these actions don't occur as personal tasks. They simply keep in place the agreements that the business has with its client.

Decision-making, planning, implementation, and negotiation all will be very different experiences for you, and new possibilities will emerge, when you see them as the business's actions.

When you break free from limiting conversations, you can begin to view your business as something far greater than just a way to make a living. It becomes a vehicle to contribute to your community and the world. It becomes a platform for the legacy that you're creating.

And importantly, it persistently reveals its potential to be an asset of real value. Your asset of value! When you see it this way—separate from you but guided by your word—everything changes.

In our workshops we exclaim "pineapple!" to represent this collapse of self with business. It's a fun reminder when we hear people speaking from "I", "Me", or "Mine." This playful intervention helps reveal this habit that so many people are blind to—the fusing of our personal identity with that of business. In *Pineapple and Profits*, we'll call this practice collapsing contexts. It severely limits what's possible for you and for your business.

What keeps your business small?

Have you ever considered what keeps a small business small? We suggest in this book that there are two possibilities to reflect on:

- Collapsing contexts—collapsing your personal identity with your business
- The limiting beliefs you then bring to these collapsed contexts

You might think your business has not grown as much as it could have because of a lack of capital. Or market conditions. Or competition. And indeed, these can be factors. But after working with thousands of small business owners, we've discovered something surprising: the biggest constraints aren't external, they're internal. They're how you talk to yourself and others about what's possible for you and your business.

In addition to emphasizing collapsing contexts, *Pineapple and Profits* focuses especially on limiting beliefs that show up in conversations about money and finance that can keep you and your business from achieving extraordinary success.

The cost of collapsing you and your business

When business owners blur the lines between themselves and their business, the consequences show up everywhere. Business owners:

- Make less objective decisions
- Struggle to define roles (owner, director, manager, employee)
- Undervalue their own time
- Work in the business instead of on the business
- Never truly switch off, leading to exhaustion
- Fail to model healthy behaviors, such as taking vacation
- Don't recognize their business as an asset of value
- Struggle with exit planning and business valuation

One of the signs that you are collapsing your own identity with that of the business is the sort of statements you make—consciously and unconsciously—about yourself and your work in the business.

Do you hear yourself saying statements like these about yourself?:

- "I'm too busy to work on building the business."
- "Nobody can do it as well as me."
- "I can't do any more."
- "I'm not good enough."
- "I have to work hard for every dollar."
- "I don't deserve success or wealth."
- "I just can't get ahead."
- "You can't count on other people."
- "I'm not good at math."
- "I'm just trying to make a living."
- "I'm better than other people."
- "Other people are better than me."

You might find yourself making similar limiting comments about the business:

- "I need to check the bank balance before paying myself."
- "There's never enough money."

- "The more I make, the more I spend."
- "I want to grow, but I can't afford it, and I don't want any more debt."

These thoughts can hold you back. But once you recognize them, you can replace them with more constructive thoughts—statements to yourself that are rooted in the context of you and your business as separate entities.

As a first step to uproot these limiting beliefs, listen to what you say to yourself, both publicly and privately. Do you see the collapse?

Limiting personal conversations often keep both you and your business small; they can prevent you from being fully responsible for your success as a business owner *and* the success of your business.

How a business owner (with a healthy separate identity) talks

In contrast, successful business owners with a healthy separation between themselves and their business hear themselves asking questions like:

- "Will this decision increase the exit valuation of my business?"
- "What systems can I introduce so we can scale more easily?"
- "Remember to sell to existing clients."
- "Have we been asking our clients for introductions and references?"
- "Is this decision in line with our business plan?"
- "What are the quarterly financial reports saying about this line of business? Is the revenue growing, and is this product profitable?"
- "What can we do to make this more efficient?"
- "Why are our monthly accounts not ready by the seventh of the following month?"
- "What partnerships and joint ventures could expand our reach?"

These questions are driven by their focus on what matters to the business such as:

- Focusing on building an asset of value

- Identifying business growth and value engines
- Prioritizing client retention and acquisition
- Making decisions based on strategy and financial reporting
- Developing operating systems
- Maintaining structured financial reporting
- Different opportunities for growth

When you make the shift of separating yourself from your business, you gain:

- **More objective decision-making:** You step outside of personal limitations and focus on what's best for the business as a whole.
- **A clearer financial strategy:** Viewing your business as an asset allows you to plan for growth, sustainability, and even an exit strategy.
- **New opportunities:** A broader perspective opens up avenues for financing, delegation, and strategic partnerships.
- **Long-term sustainability:** Your business can take care of you, your employees, and stakeholders in a way that extends beyond your personal effort.

New opportunities emerge when you begin to see your business as an entity separate from yourself. When you and your business have healthy separate identities, the business will no longer face limitations from your own personal skill set, doubts, or fears. You will also feel less pressure and stress, leading to a cycle of better decisions and conversations. Instead of thinking, "Can I handle this?" you begin to ask, "What does the business need?" You start making decisions from the standpoint of building something bigger than yourself... maybe beyond the bounds of your personal identity.

You find yourself working on a business that can grow, evolve, and thrive beyond your personal limitations. When you embrace the separation between you and your business, you open the door to greater success, more freedom, and a healthier relationship with yourself and with your company.

In the chapters that follow, we'll build on this foundation of healthy separation. We'll give you tools and knowledge to grow your business into the valuable asset it can be.

SEPARATION CASE STUDY:

"This is going to change my life."

Here's an example of applying the pineapple concept. A few years ago, Peter delivered a workshop to micro-entrepreneurs in eSwatini, a small landlocked country in Southern Africa.

During a discussion about the importance of viewing a business as separate from its owner, he witnessed the transformative power of this concept.

One participant, a dressmaker who owned two sewing machines and wanted to expand her business, had always struggled with saving money. As a respected community leader, she felt obligated when people in her village asked for financial help for funerals and medical emergencies. This made saving money and growing the business difficult.

When she grasped the pineapple concept, she exclaimed, "Oh wow, this is going to change my life!"

She explained, "Now I can say no. I can tell people, 'I don't have any money.' And when they say, 'But we see your clients coming and going,' I can respond, 'That's not my money, it's the business's money.'"

ACTION STEPS

Reflect and write down your answers to these questions regarding your experience as a business owner:

- What is it like to be you, the business owner, day to day?
- What challenges are you currently facing?
- What matters most to you about your business?
- Where do you feel stuck or overwhelmed?
- What isn't happening in your business that you want to happen?
- How would you describe your overall experience of business ownership?

KEY TAKEAWAYS

- Begin noticing the collapse between yourself and your business.
- Look for ways that this collapse limits what's possible for your and the business.
- Practice shifting from "I am the business" to "I own the business." Recognize your business as a separate entity to gain objectivity, clearer financial strategy, and access to new opportunities and long-term sustainability.

Peter video

Kelly video

TESTIMONIAL

> **"**
>
> *Giving another point of view for the business and myself was definitely an eye opener. It is a great way to view the business in other ways and change perspective on how to view yourself and the business.*
>
> - Jane L., Business Owner

2

A common limiting belief: numbers and finance

We've suggested that there are two significant reasons owner-operated businesses stay small:

- Personal limiting beliefs of the owner
- Collapsing of your personal identity with the business's identity

Our research tells us that for many business owners, it is limiting beliefs and ways of talking about numbers, money, and finance that are the major blocks to managing their business for faster growth and greater success. There are other barriers in people's thinking of course, but in this book, we focus on the money-related limiting conversations.

Consider what happens when you look at your financial statements. Does your chest tighten? Do you feel that familiar wave of confusion? Do you tell yourself, "I'm just not a numbers person?"

If this is your experience, know that these aren't character flaws. They're past-based beliefs that quietly run your business without you even realizing it.

Kelly's experience

Kelly discovered this truth the hard way. At eight years old, she got a lower grade in math. That single grade became an unquestioned truth: "I'm not a math person." For decades, that belief shaped every math class and, later in life, every financial decision, every avoided spreadsheet, every delegated—or abdicated—

responsibility. Kelly became an expert in her field but always felt like she was driving with the parking brake on when it came to business and finance.

As a financial educator and coach, Peter saw this pattern everywhere—business owners who were brilliant at their craft but terrified of their numbers. He knew finance wasn't about being good at math; it was about understanding a language. So he created visual and plain-language tools to make business finance accessible to everyone.

Peter and Kelly met in 2016 when Peter brought his team to a leadership workshop Kelly was delivering in Vancouver, Canada. At the end of the program, Peter approached Kelly with a simple observation: "I think we can do some great things together." He invited her to experience his Color Accounting™ program to see if there were synergies between their two methods.

When their paths crossed, something clicked. Kelly attended Peter's course expecting to endure another boring finance seminar. Within an hour, she had a powerful insight. The problem wasn't her ability, it was a 40-year-old limiting belief about math that she'd never questioned and had evolved into a limiting conversation about finance. That moment changed everything. Fast-forward, and Kelly and Peter have helped hundreds of business owners have similar breakthrough insights.

We invite you to examine your own relationship with numbers and finance. If you're like many small business owners, you might think, "I rely on my employee to tell me about our finances," or "I've always depended on someone else to handle the numbers." Maybe you've never really looked at the financial side of your business. If that sounds familiar, once again, you're not alone.

So many business owners master their fields—whether as property investors, doctors, realtors, veterinarians, dog groomers, or attorneys. They excel in their technical expertise, but when it comes to running a business, they find themselves in uncharted territory. Business ownership demands an entirely different skill set, one that importantly includes financial literacy and strategic decision-making.

Your discovery of your relationship with finance and numbers starts with reflection—taking an honest inventory of how you currently engage with the financial side of your business. By the end of your discovery journey, you'll gain a new appreciation for your role as a business owner.

This book offers an opportunity to pause, reflect, and be entirely honest with yourself about what it means to be a business owner. It also provides a chance to examine how finance fits into your overall vision. More importantly, it's about being authentic with yourself regarding the challenges and responsibilities that come with building a business.

I see a zebra!

A participant in one of Peter's workshops made an offhand but actually quite profound comment. She managed a nonprofit business in Washington, D.C. and was deeply committed to her work, yet she knew she needed to understand the financial side of the operations. Nonprofit finances can be more complicated than for-profit businesses because donors often attach strings to their money, creating additional restrictions that need careful tracking.

When reflecting on her relationship with finance, she blurted, "When I see a balance sheet, I see a zebra." The comment was impromptu yet perfectly descriptive of her visceral response. The balance sheet bewildered her. The dense stripes of rows and columns, the mix of familiar and strange jumbled with numbers, much of it ambiguous. Where does one even begin?!

"Zebra" captured her confusion perfectly. A zebra's stripes exist to confuse predators. Lions find it harder to pick out their individual prey from the moving herd. Where does the head start and the tail end? How big is that vulnerable calf? And the flies don't know where to land.

Financial reports create this same confusion and bewilderment for many people. "Where do I start?" you might ask yourself. We use shapes and color to make financial statements more intuitive, removing the confusion so you know exactly what you're looking at and where to begin.

What's your relationship to numbers and finance?

Balance sheet

ASSETS

Current assets

Cash & deposits	46,000
Accounts receivable	128,000
Inventories	239,000
Total current assets	413,000

Non-current assets

Land & buildings	502,000
Equipment, fixtures & fittings	177,000
Investment in other companies	1,000
Total non-current assets	680,000
TOTAL ASSETS	**1,093,000**

LIABILITIES

Current liabilities

Borrowings	64,000
Payables	182,000
Total current liabilities	246,000

Non-current liabilities

Borrowings	548,000
Provisions	30,000
Total non-current liabilities	578,000
TOTAL LIABILITIES	**824,000**
NET ASSETS	**269,000**

EQUITY

Issued capital	192,000
Retained earnings	77,000
TOTAL EQUITY	**269,000**
TOTAL LIABILITIES AND EQUITY	**1,093,000**

Income statement

Sales	**1,457,000**
Less: cost of sales	
Cost of sales (COS)	1,136,000
Gross profit	**321,000**
Less: operating expenses	
Accounting & bookkeeping	8,000
Advertising	6,000
Bank charges	3,000
Depreciation	29,000
Employment expenses	145,000
Insurance	28,000
Rental of office equipment	2,000
Sponsorships	3,000
Telephone & utilities	9,000
Other	18,000
Total operating expenses	*251,000*
Operating profit	**70,000**
Interest expense	15,000
Profit before tax	**55,000**
Less: income tax expenses	17,000
Profit for the period	**38,000**

ACTION STEPS

Kelly video

1. Look at the sample financial reports on the previous page and write down your honest reactions and thoughts.
   - What comes up for you?
   - What feelings arise?
   - What is your relationship with finance and with financial reports?
2. Think about your business:
   - How do you feel when dealing with money and finance in your business?
   - What beliefs do you hold about money and financial management?
   - How comfortable are you with making financial decisions?
   - How much time do you spend understanding your business finances?
   - What does financial success look like to you?

KEY TAKEAWAYS

- **Question your existing beliefs:** Look at the deeply ingrained thoughts about your abilities, money, or success, and question whether they truly serve you.
- **Listen to yourself:** Pay attention to what you say to yourself, both publicly and privately, to become more aware of what's influencing you and your business.

TESTIMONIAL

> **"**
> *Pineapple was the light bulb moment for me. It's still the lightbulb moment for me, and I'm still trying to work on it and implement it, because I have my personal hat on, and now I'm growing into my business hat. I am an employee of the business. The business is not me. I need to act accordingly and make sure that I am delegating tasks and responsibilities accordingly, and that's my takeaway.* - Doreen S., Small Business Owner

3

Learning any skill starts with language

Imagine learning a new sport, a musical instrument, or even becoming a doctor or lawyer. The first step is always learning the words and ideas used in that field. In other words, learning the language. The same goes for business:

- Learn the words
- Practice using them
- Get comfortable in that world

Many vocations, like sports, music, law, or business, have their own "language" and ways of thinking. They each have particular words, ways of using those words, special meanings for the words, meanings that differ from everyday usage, and linguistic conventions.

Our "Investing In Your Future" course, which gave rise to this book, approaches business finance and leadership through the lens of language. The course is all about helping you become a better business owner and leader. In it, we look at how you think and talk about finance and your business, both out loud and in your own head. The learning we want for you isn't just facts or even your ability to simply read and interpret those facts; it's about actually changing what you do. Yes, we address how finance works because knowing how is a big part of understanding business, but we go a step further. We look at how you work and behave with your knowledge and understanding.

An important tool we use to do this is a special **communication model**.

A communication model is just a fancy way of saying, "The set of words, ideas, and rules we use to talk about something."

Think of it as a pair of glasses that helps you see and make sense of business and financial topics. Different lenses give you different views. For business and finance, the words you use and the way you use them matter. Those who get good at business get comfortable speaking its language, feeling at home operating within its grammar, vocabulary, and syntax.

Communication model

The color palette to the left is a visual representation of our communication model that we call the BaSIS Board™. You'll see a version of it later with numbers and words on it that derive from the **Ba**lance **S**heet and **I**ncome **S**tatement (BaSIS) financial reports. But it's not just about the numbers that will fill it; this communication model is very much about the story of your business. You'll see how the parts combine to create a value-narrative of the business. When you look at an income statement or balance sheet, consider that you're actually looking at parts of the communication model that help you understand and see your business in a new way.

Consider that the diagram above represents the world of accounting. The top three boxes are a snapshot of your business—what it has and who it has made promises to. Those boxes represent a balance sheet. The bottom two boxes show how your business is performing—what it's doing to fulfill those promises. Like a financial video of your business, those bottom two boxes represent an income statement. We'll label the five boxes with the key terms revenue, equity, liabilities, assets and expenses. And stepping back to see the diagram as two columns, the three right-hand orange boxes inform the two left-hand green boxes. We'll label these sources and uses. The five boxes of the model capture everything that happens in your business. Nothing about your business's finances escapes their reach. Nothing else is needed other than these five elements. Understanding them will enable you to think more clearly about your business and make better decisions.

Understanding them requires you to appreciate three aspects of the model: The meaning of the five boxes, how they connect and relate to each other, and how they get filled with numbers. We call these three aspects language, structure, and logic.

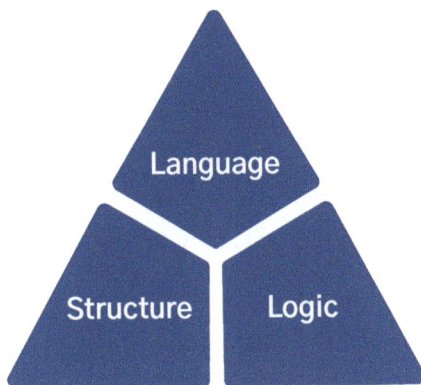

Language: The words and what they specifically mean in the communication model. You've likely heard many of these terms before, but they are often poorly explained and widely misunderstood.

Structure: This dimension focuses on how financial information and reports are organized. For example, why does a balance sheet have two sides? Where does the income statement fit in relation to the balance sheet?

Logic: This is about increases and decreases in the accounts. When something happens in your business, it has two impacts. These impacts must either both increase, both decrease, or cancel each other out when one increases and the other decreases.

When you get these three things—language, structure, and logic—accounting and finance become intuitive and logical to understand in the same way that humans intuitively understand folklore or any other stories that similarly have a language, structure, and internal logic.

What this means is, when you look at a traditional balance sheet and income statement, like those shown below, they too tell an intuitive story. Shown below with colors green and orange, they present the same information as the communication model, just laid out differently.

The story of your business

Balance sheet

ASSETS	
Current assets	
Cash & deposits	46,000
Accounts receivable	128,000
Inventories	239,000
Total current assets	413,000
Non-current assets	
Land & buildings	502,000
Equipment, fixtures & fittings	177,000
Investment in other companies	1,000
Total non-current assets	680,000
TOTAL ASSETS	**1,093,000**

LIABILITIES	
Current liabilities	
Borrowings	64,000
Payables	182,000
Total current liabilities	246,000
Non-current liabilities	
Borrowings	548,000
Provisions	30,000
Total non-current liabilities	578,000
TOTAL LIABILITIES	**824,000**
NET ASSETS	**269,000**
EQUITY	
Issued capital	192,000
Retained earnings	77,000
TOTAL EQUITY	**269,000**
TOTAL LIABILITIES AND EQUITY	**1,093,000**

Income statement

Sales	**1,457,000**

Less: cost of sales	
Cost of sales (COS)	1,136,000

Gross profit	**321,000**

Less: operating expenses

Accounting & bookkeeping	8,000
Advertising	6,000
Bank charges	3,000
Depreciation	29,000
Employment expenses	145,000
Insurance	28,000
Rental of office equipment	2,000
Sponsorships	3,000
Telephone & utilities	9,000
Other	18,000
Total operating expenses	*251,000*

Operating profit	**70,000**

Interest expense	15,000

Profit before tax	**55,000**

Less: income tax expenses	17,000

Profit for the period	**38,000**

A lack of accounting literacy limits your financial literacy and business acumen. To increase your business skills, you must increase your financial literacy.

Notice what comes up for you when we say this.

At this point, you might think, "Oh no! Is my business acumen really limited by my knowledge of accounting? Because accounting is awful ... I've heard it from others." You are not wrong; accounting has a bad reputation. Maybe you remember struggling with it in school, finding it confusing and frustrating.

But here's the opportunity: While we've found accounting literacy is an underappreciated foundation of financial literacy, we've also found that the key to more rapidly and easily becoming accounting literate is to approach it as a language, through a communication lens. Enter the communication model.

When you learn to operate inside of the communication model, a whole new understanding of finance intuitively opens up, and you begin to see your business in a new way. Your natural grasp of the language, structure, and the logic of the communication model will give you a powerful view of your business from which to make decisions and operate.

Pulling together the concepts of the communication model and pineapple, we can now see that when you are collapsing your personal identity with your business identity, you are not speaking the language of business. And that's not good for you or your business.

Accounting is a 500-year-old communication model

Despite its reputation as boring or difficult, accounting stands as one of humanity's most important social technologies. It's so deeply embedded in our daily lives that we barely notice it—it's the water that fish never discover. Accounting is everywhere and enables everything from catching a bus to renting or buying a home, supporting a charity, or managing your savings.

Alongside literacy and numeracy, accounting ranks as one of civilization's three most transformative social technologies. Archaeological evidence suggests accounting practices have existed for nearly 10,000 years, predating written language in many societies.

Double-entry bookkeeping—accounting in its refined form—is a relatively recent innovation, dating back to at least the 13th century. It became widely known through *Summa de Arithmetica, Geometria, Proportioni et Proportionalità (Summary of Arithmetic, Geometry, Proportions, and Proportionality)*, published by Luca Pacioli in 1494. His method of recording transactions on both sides of a ledger created a system that has remained essentially unchanged for more than 500 years.

Understanding this powerful legacy helps you appreciate what accounting can do for your business today.

What is accounting?

By definition, accounting draws on the root of "count," which reflects that numbers are involved. But surprisingly, understanding accounting is as much about words as numbers. While numbers ultimately reveal performance and quantity, understanding accounting begins with language along with the two other dimensions that go with language: structure and logic.

At its essence, accounting is simply a sophisticated system of sorting and grouping.

Think about how sorting improves your daily life: separating clean clothes from dirty clothes helps you manage laundry, while grouping customer payments by due date helps you manage cash flow. In your kitchen, you organize cookware, dishes, and utensils, creating logical groups and subgroups that make sense to you.

Accounting works the same way. You categorize expenses as financial or operational, further dividing operational costs into staff, supplies, and utilities. The specifics of these subgroups remain flexible and up to you.

However, one crucial rule exists: never mix up the five main categories in the communication model. It's like the fundamental rooms in a house—kitchens, bedrooms, and bathrooms serve distinct purposes that everyone recognizes. Similarly, accounting has five "rooms" that maintain order and clarity.

These five absolute groups form the foundation that tells your business's complete financial story.

Chart of accounts

When setting up a business accounting system (think QuickBooks), the chart of accounts serves as the list of categories used to track business activities and assets.

You control this system. Just as you organize your kitchen in a way that makes sense to you, you design your accounting structure to fit your business needs. If you're a baker and want to track your cookie supply, you create an account for cookies, with as much detail as you like. You might even create sub-accounts for chocolate cookies and vanilla cookies.

The purpose of this system is to provide useful information for decision-making. At home, you might use a laundry basket to determine when it's time to do the washing. In business, tracking accounts receivable helps you decide when to focus on collecting payments rather than making new sales.

Too much detail costs time to maintain and increases the risk of errors. But too little detail can leave you without the information needed to make informed decisions. You decide how many account categories to use and what to call them. While naming conventions exist, such as "accounts receivable" or its synonym "trade debtors," your choices should reflect both your needs and the needs of financial report users. For instance, the Internal Revenue Service requires businesses to track entertainment expenses separately since they are not fully tax deductible. That said, don't let external requirements dictate your entire system— your chart of accounts exists to serve you, not the other way around.

While you have flexibility in designing your system, certain top-level categories remain absolute and immutable. Remember, only five categories exist. You only need to learn the structure, language, and logic of each.

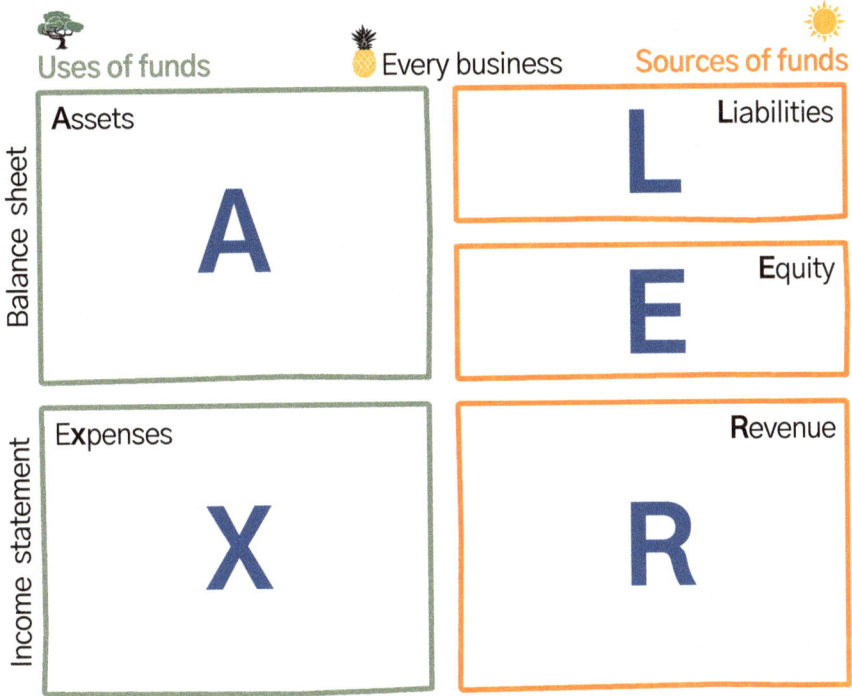

We use the mnemonic **RELAX** to remember them:

- **Revenue**
- **Equity**
- **Liabilities**
- **Assets**
- **eXpenses**

All financial information falls into one of these five categories. We call them the five boxes.

- The top three show what your business owns and owes. These become the **balance sheet**.
- The bottom two show how your business is performing. They become the **income statement**.

Everything about your business's finances fits into these five blocks. Under-

25

standing them means you can make smarter decisions.

The three orange boxes represent sources of energy. Notice the sun at the top right. In the bottom-right-hand corner, you can see *revenue*. Selling fruits and vegetables is just one example of revenue. For a marketing agency, delivering an advertising campaign would be a revenue source. The orange box in the middle is *equity*, which is the business's promise to its owner. And most businesses are funded in part by lenders and creditors. There are *liabilities* and debts to banks and credit card companies. The obligations to them are shown in the top-right orange box.

The green boxes on the left show how the energy is used. Notice the tree that's "grown" using the sunshine. The business has *assets*, which is the top green box on the left, and the business has *expenses* because it uses workers paid through salaries, consumes electricity and utilities, and so on.

To describe any business, only these five categories are needed. There are no other categories. And that's what accounting is—it's just a way of sorting information into groups so you can make good sense of it. We'll practice describing business transactions and scenarios using the BaSIS Board and its five boxes later. Fun!

Recapping pineapple

Everyone has their own "lens" on the world and how they talk about what matters to them. If you bring your personal worries or doubts (like "I'm just not good with numbers") into the business world, you limit yourself.

Instead, try stepping into the language of business and finance, like learning a new language. The more you use it, the more natural it will feel.

When you say things like, "I'm not good at numbers," that's your personal language creeping in. Accounting and finance are just languages you can learn. There's no need to fear them; they're your tools for running a successful business.

So, the main point: **Get comfortable using the language of business and finance.** It will open up new opportunities for you and your company!

Accounting and finance

Accounting is about understanding the state of your business—the facts of where it's at and what it's been doing. You may not like where it's at or be happy with what it's achieved, but what's important is to accept what's in front of you. We call this "what's so." Accounting provides this financial clarity.

Think of your business as a whole. At the center is accounting, and surrounding it is the broader world of finance.

Finance is the energy of your business.

Accounting, shown at the heart of the wheel, captures, structures, and records the finances of the business. Those finances are the sources of the business's assets that enable the business's engagement with the outside world. The business uses the assets to achieve its purpose and serve its owners.

Just as energy powers the human body, finances power your business. Without it, or with a shortage of it, everything slows down. Decision-making stalls. Growth stagnates. But when you understand and harness finance, you create momentum. You gain access to new opportunities, stronger decision-making, and the ability to scale your business in ways that were previously unimaginable.

So, the question becomes, "How are you managing your business's energy?"

By using accounting to get clear on your financial reality—by understanding your numbers, cash flow, and financial structures—you gain greater access to building a business that thrives in the real world. And when you do that, you move from being in your business to truly owning it.

Your business as a whole

Picture a wheel with different spokes. Each spoke stands for a part of your business: HR, marketing, sales, operations, and so on. The center of the wheel is **accounting and finance**, with language that connects to and enables every other aspect of your business.

Why accounting and finance matter

Accounting and finance are related, but not the same thing.

- **Finance** is about managing money.
- **Accounting** is about tracking what's happening with that money.

If you want to get better at business, you have to get comfortable with both. The more you understand accounting, the easier it is to make good business decisions.

Tracking the business energy: The accounting duality

As a business owner, understanding accounting duality is essential because it allows you to see the complete financial picture of your business, how the business sourced energy, and what it's using that energy for.

A business is all about achieving its goals using the assets financed by the business's funders. Inherent in the very design of accounting is the mechanism to track those two aspects of business—the sources of the assets and the use of the assets. The recording of these two aspects of business is what we call the accounting duality.

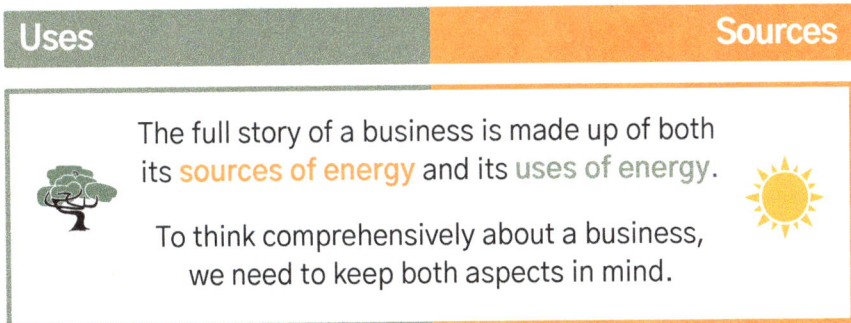

Uses		Sources

The full story of a business is made up of both its sources of energy and its uses of energy.

To think comprehensively about a business, we need to keep both aspects in mind.

In the next chapter, we'll see how this task of capturing the business's use of energy shows up in the design of that key financial report, the balance sheet.

TESTIMONIAL

"

One of the biggest breakthroughs in that course is that we got that the business is its own entity. And the job of the business is to make money for us. So, that literally altered everything for me. I was looking at it like the business is me.

- Jackie L., Real Estate Professional

4

The balance sheet: A butterfly

The balance sheet is the central financial report that tells us "what's so" or the reality about the position of any business. The balance sheet tells us what assets the business was using at a particular date and how it financed those assets. In other words, the sources of business energy and the uses of the business energy.

The metaphor of a butterfly illustrates the two sides of the balance sheet:

- The orange, right-hand wing of the butterfly shows the **sources** of the business's assets as well as from whom and how they were acquired. They were acquired by making promises to lenders and investors, so that's what the right-hand-side of the balance sheet shows: promises or obligations.
- The green, left-hand-side of the butterfly shows the assets that were acquired by making the promises. It shows the **use** to which the funding energy was put.

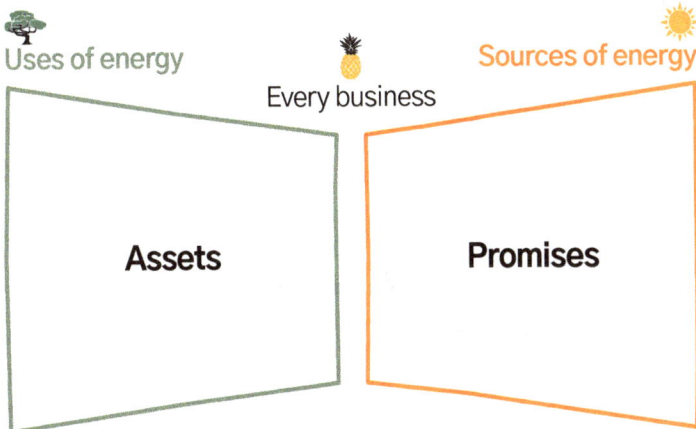

Uses of energy   Sources of energy

Every business

Assets   Promises

We mentioned earlier that funding is the energy that drives a business—it's the life force of a business. Funding is broader than money, which is why we consider it energy. If you've ever taken a course in economics, you know that there are various definitions of money. The narrowest definition is the money you have in your pocket; in a broader context, money includes credit and the like.

Let's revisit our fictional business, Alicia's Organic Market, and look at its balance sheet. You see the pineapple symbol to remind us of whose point of view we're examining. Besides Alicia's Organic Market, there are other entities involved in the story, such as Alicia herself, who owns the actual business, and the lender, who loans money to the business.

Just as a butterfly needs both wings to fly, a business requires both sources and uses of funds. The right wing captures where the energy (funding) comes from, while the left wing shows how that energy is used.

Uses of energy — Alicia's Organic Market — Sources of energy

Assets

Liabilities
Promises to lenders

Equity
Promises to owners

The three elements shown in the butterfly are the top three elements you met in the last chapter in the "color palette" communication model. We remember its five elements with the mnemonic RELAX. What you're seeing in the butterfly above are the "ELA" part of the board, the top three boxes.

Communication model

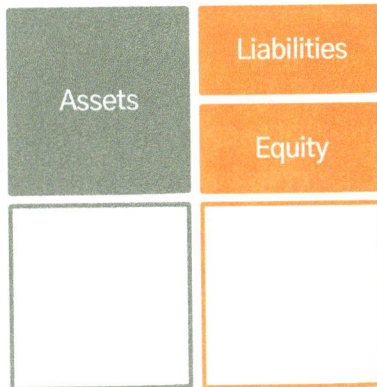

You're probably noticing that we haven't really talked about numbers yet. Getting to grips with accounting is much more about language, structure, and logic than numbers. Once you understand the RELAX framework, you begin to hear your business speak.

Three aspects of the RELAX framework

We mentioned in chapter 3 that there are three aspects of the RELAX framework. Let's examine this further.

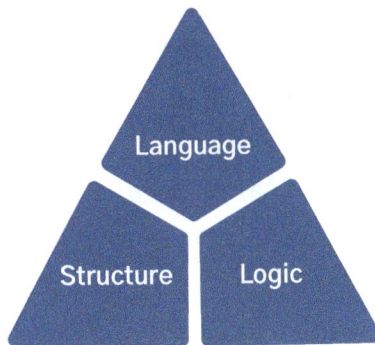

Language: The specialized terms that describe what's happening in your business. Revenue isn't money coming in, it's value-generating activity. Equity isn't ownership, it's the business's promise to you, the owner.

Structure: The RELAX model gives you a complete view. The top three elements (assets, liabilities, equity) show your position—where you are. The bottom two (revenue, expenses) show your performance—how you got there.

Logic: The ups and downs that happen in the framework when the business transacts. You'll discover that every business transaction has two impacts on the framework, always maintaining the balance of the butterfly.

Together, these create a communication model. By addressing these three aspects, you'll be able to participate in financial conversations with confidence. That access means power.

Assets: Where all the value lies

Let's take a closer look at the three components that make up the butterfly that is the balance sheet. We'll start by exploring assets. We'll get clear on what an asset is, how we classify them, and how we measure them.

Definition of an asset

Intuitively, we recognize an asset when we see one. Nevertheless, it's useful to be explicit about what makes an asset uniquely an asset. An asset is anything that's valuable. Being valuable is the unique quality of assets. Nothing else in accounting and finance is—neither revenue, expenses, liabilities, nor equity are valuable. Only assets have value.

> ### ANYTHING VALUABLE IS AN ASSET

To be valuable typically means having qualities such as being useful, being able to be swapped for money, being capable of generating more assets, being sellable, and being capable of settling a debt. However, not all assets are sellable. If you have a college degree, it's a qualification that's attached to you and can't be sold. The same with your reputation. Both are assets, though neither is sellable. And, of course, you can't hand over your reputation to pay your credit card debt.

Showing and not showing assets on the balance sheet

Assets are recorded on one side of the balance sheet. But in order to be shown, the asset must be measurable <u>and</u> it must be controlled by the business. These are what we call asset recognition criteria. The requirements mean that balance sheets don't show all of a business's assets, because some aren't measurable, and some don't belong to the business (such as a beautiful view in front of a restaurant or a parking lot adjacent to a store).

What drives these "measurable" and "controlled" reporting criteria is the need to make the information on the balance sheet relevant and reliable. If we just guessed at the value of assets, that information wouldn't be useful.

If a business has slowly developed a reputation for excellent service over a number of years, no one can say for certain what that reputation is worth. Therefore, home-grown reputation isn't shown on a balance sheet. On the other hand, if a business buys another business and pays for its reputation, then that reputation is recorded (as "acquired goodwill"). How much the business paid for the reputation becomes its measured worth.

Because of the reporting criteria, sometimes the most important and valuable assets of a business aren't listed. For example, Coca-Cola's brand name isn't on Coca-Cola's balance sheet, because no one knows exactly what it's worth. The stock market forms an opinion on its worth, and that is reflected in the share price of Coca-Cola, but not on the balance sheet. The market valuation and the "book value" of Coca-Cola are different because of all the unreported assets it has.

Why should you consider the assets that are recognized and unrecognized on a balance sheet?

We want you to think about the whole of your business. Having the point of view—remember the pineapple!—that comes from standing back from your business with a perspective that provides access to different decisions. You can clearly see the assets of the business, and clearly seeing the fullness of what sits on the left-hand side of that butterfly matters significantly.

CASE STUDY:

Recognizing hidden assets

Peter had a colleague whose daughter was dating a wonderful man who didn't want to get married because he had student debt. He felt badly about bringing debt into the marriage and wanted to pay off his student debt first. The man's future father-in-law said, "No, you're forgetting what you have on the green wing of the butterfly. You have this asset called all your knowledge and an MBA." After hearing that, the world occurred differently to the young man. He proposed literally the next week because he knew he wasn't just sitting with debt. He knew he had an asset that was appreciating—his knowledge—and he was bringing that asset into the marriage as well.

When you start to examine recognized and unrecognized assets, you discover significant value in understanding what's possible for the business, and maybe even what's missing that needs to be added when you're looking from the view of your business.

Classifying assets

Assets divide into several categories:

- **Cash:** Cash in the bank or on-hand is an asset that takes up a lot of management's time—making sure there's enough of it and managing the timing and rate of cash flowing into and out of the business.
- **Tangible assets:** Physical items such as buildings, equipment, and furniture.
- **Intangible assets:** Nonphysical assets like patents, trademarks, and brand reputation.
- **Recognized assets:** Items formally recorded on the balance sheet, such as cash and inventory and those mentioned above.

- **Unrecognized assets:** Valuable elements not captured in financial statements, like customer loyalty or company culture.

Recognized
Shown on the balance sheet

Unrecognized
Not shown on the balance sheet

	Recognized	Unrecognized
Tangible Can touch these	• Shelving • Point of sale equipment • Supplies • Building (owned) • Vehicles (owned)	• Neighborhood • Nearby parking • Interstate access • Building (rented) • Vehicles (rented)
Intangible Can't touch these	• Accounting receivable • Trademarks • Purchased goodwill	• Extended trading hours • Customer service • Generated goodwill

Other categories of assets

Let's examine some intangible assets that might appear on a balance sheet.

- **Deposits:** If you have paid a deposit on a lease, for example, that deposit is an asset, because you have the right to get it back.
- **Accounts receivable:** Do you like being owed money? The answer should be yes! Being owed money is the next best thing to actually having cash. While you may prefer to have the money in hand, being owed money is better than not being owed money. It's a valuable claim, which is an asset.
- **Intellectual property:** If you have intellectual property, such as a recognizable brand name or logo, this can be a valuable intangible asset.

CASE STUDY:

The hidden asset that changed everything

A dog groomer in our program complained about barely breaking even despite being fully booked. When asked about unrecognized assets, she mentioned offhandedly that she knew every dog's name and their owners' vacation schedules.

This was gold. She leveraged this knowledge to:

- Create a VIP notification system for last-minute openings
- Offer vacation boarding services
- Partner with a local pet photographer for holiday cards

Her "worthless" customer knowledge became a $30,000 annual revenue stream. The asset was always there, she just hadn't recognized it.

ACTION STEP

List three unrecognized assets in your business. How might you leverage them more fully this quarter?

TESTIMONIAL

"

I am able to look at the financials without getting scared. I think this was a great start for me building my business. - Pritika G., Business Owner

Measuring assets

There is no singular truth about the value of an asset. The number that is "pinned" on an asset on the balance sheet is informed by, and arrived at, by considering a number of factors. They can be measured in different ways, including:

- **Historical cost:** The price paid for an asset.
- **Market value:** The price at which an asset could be sold on an active market.
- **Fair value:** The amount for which two reasonable people would agree to exchange the asset.
- **Replacement cost:** The cost to replace the asset.
- **Present value:** The current worth of future cash flows; the right to receive cash in the future.
- **Realizable value:** The amount that the seller could get for the asset under the circumstances, which might be a liquidation event where "everything must go," and which amount could be reduced by an agent's commission. The amount might be less than the normal market value.

Sources of energy: How the business gets assets

Every business starts with no assets ... an empty vessel. Then the business sources assets in three possible ways: it can make a promise to a lender, make a promise to an owner (investor), or it can serve a client in return for payment. The promises are recorded on the balance sheet. The servicing of clients is recorded in the income statement.

- **Liabilities:** When a lender provides an asset, the business promises to return it (and some more, for interest). That promise or obligation appears as a liability on the balance sheet.
- **Equity:** When an owner (investor) provides an asset to the business, the business promises to use it, grow it, and eventually return it to that owner. That promise appears as equity on the balance sheet.
- **Revenue:** The third source of funds for any business is serving customers.

Those service activities appear as revenue on the income statement. The revenue could be giving consulting advice, cutting hair, or providing goods. In return, customers provide assets as payments, typically cash. The assets provided by customers are promised to shareholders. Those generated promises to shareholders are reported on the balance sheet as profit within equity.

Assets = Promises

For example, if you start with $30,000 borrowed from a bank and $20,000 invested by the owner, you have $50,000 in assets.

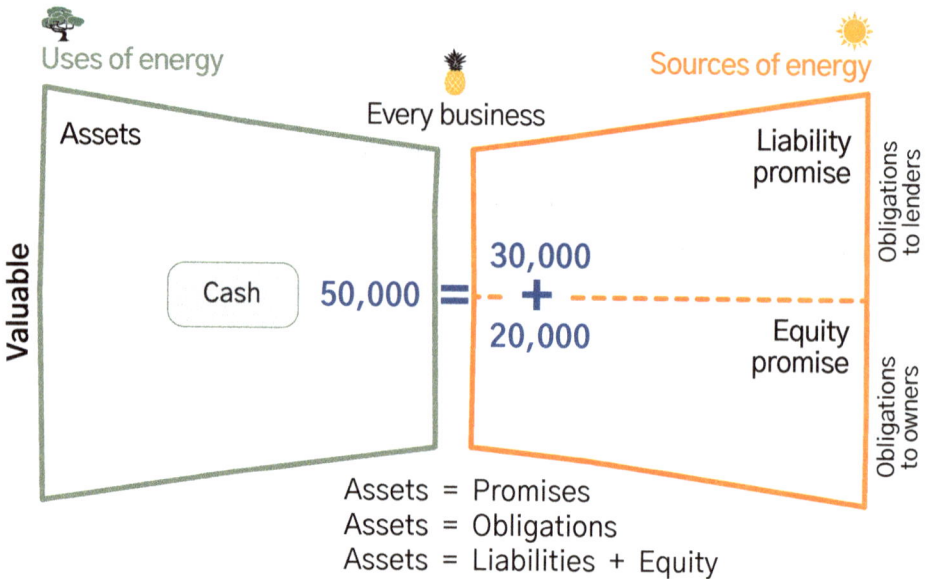

$$Cash \quad 50,000 = \frac{30,000}{20,000}$$

Assets = Promises
Assets = Obligations
Assets = Liabilities + Equity

The balance sheet above shows how the $50,000 cash that was contributed by the lenders and owners is promised back to them. This matching of value received and promises in return is reflected in the accounting equation, which is expressed in three different ways beneath the butterfly.

The business would then swap some of its cash for other assets and may look more like this butterfly on the next page.

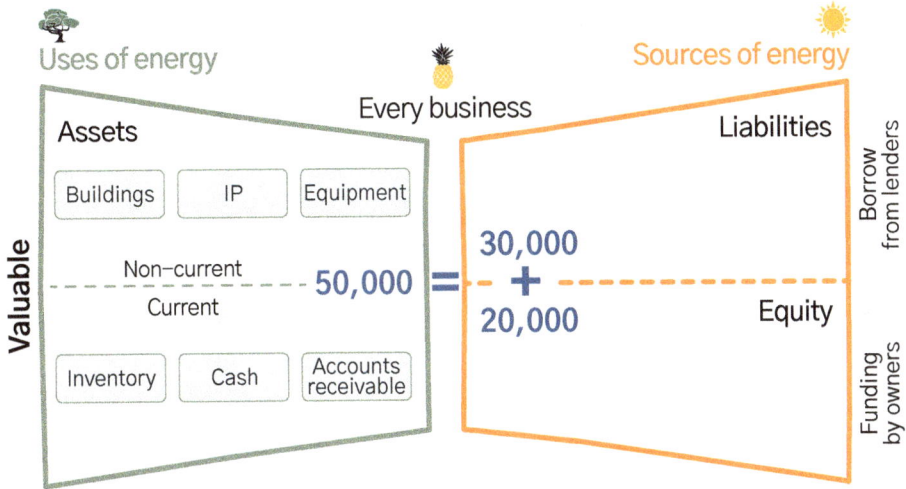

Uses of energy — Every business — Sources of energy

Assets

| Buildings | IP | Equipment |

Non–current / Current — Valuable

| Inventory | Cash | Accounts receivable |

50,000 = 30,000 + 20,000

Liabilities — Borrow from lenders

Equity — Funding by owners

A business always tries to owe the owner more. When your business generates profit, it increases its equity—meaning it owes you, the owner, more. The intention of the business is to grow the $20,000 shown above.

Balance sheet butterfly of Alicia's Organic Market

Let's see how the balance sheet of our fictional company, Alicia's Organic Market might look.

Balance sheet of:

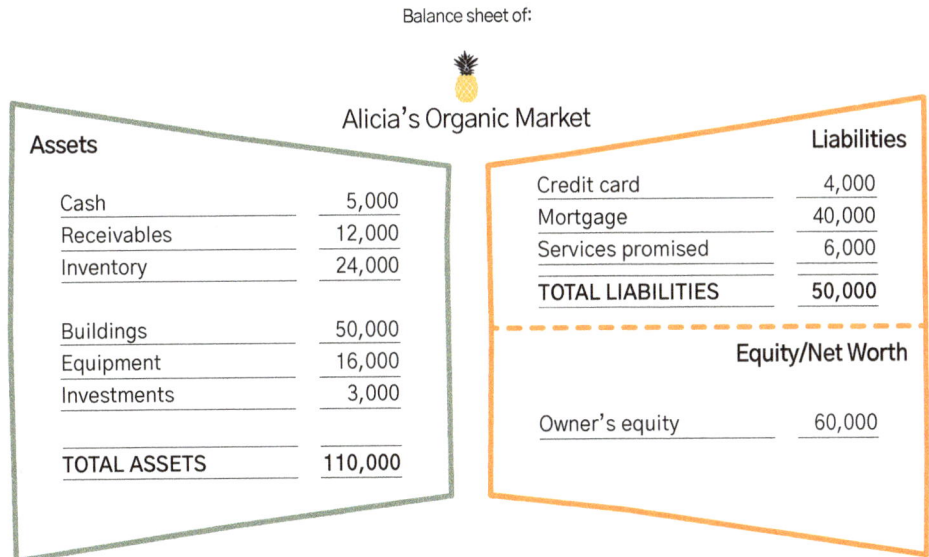

Alicia's Organic Market

Assets

Cash	5,000
Receivables	12,000
Inventory	24,000
Buildings	50,000
Equipment	16,000
Investments	3,000
TOTAL ASSETS	110,000

Liabilities

Credit card	4,000
Mortgage	40,000
Services promised	6,000
TOTAL LIABILITIES	50,000

Equity/Net Worth

| Owner's equity | 60,000 |

On the left are the assets with a total value of $110,000.

Current assets, which will be turned into cash within twelve months, are:

- Cash: money in the bank, by definition a current asset.
- Receivables: the right to be paid by customers.
- Inventory: assets held by the business for the purpose of selling to customers.

Non-current assets, which will last for more than twelve months before being used up, are:

- Buildings
- Equipment
- Investments (could be a stake in other companies)

On the other, orange, side of the balance sheet are the promises made to funders.

The liability promises to lenders and creditors amount to $50,000, meaning the business will have to give $50,000 worth of cash or services to the creditors to settle the obligations:

- Credit cards
- Bank loans
- Services promised. These are services already paid for by customers but not yet delivered to them. They are often called deferred revenue.

Let's pause on that last one. If you're a lawyer, consultant, or coach and you get paid up front, you don't record revenue when you're paid. You haven't earned the payment yet. Rather, until you have delivered the services, it's as if you've been loaned the money. You've been paid, but you still owe the delivery of service. In traditional accounting terms, services promised is called deferred revenue.

So, if a coach has received $6,000 for future coaching or services, that $6,000 is cash—an asset—that shows up on the left-hand-side of the butterfly, but it is matched on the right-hand-side by an outstanding promise to fulfill the promise. When the coaching service is delivered, the liability-promise to the customer will be canceled and replaced with an equity-promise (profit-promise) to the owner.

That's the accounting duality at work.

The balance sheet always balances. Balance means the amount of assets is the same as the amount of promises. On the left side are the assets: $110,000. We know that the liabilities amount to $50,000, and therefore, the equity total must be $60,000.

This is key: equity is always the "plug." A balance sheet always balances, because you adjust the amount of the equity to make it so. If assets drop to $90,000 and liabilities stay the same, equity becomes $40,000. That's the beauty and logic of duality.

ACTION STEP

Draw up either an imaginary balance sheet or, if you have a bookkeeper, print out your actual balance sheet. This exercise helps you visualize your butterfly—your assets and your promises.

By doing so, you'll develop a clearer understanding of how your business is structured financially and where improvements may be needed.

Balance sheet of:

Assets

Liabilities

Equity/Net Worth

How business events are recorded on the butterfly

So far we've seen how accounting is based upon a duality that capture not only what assets a business has, but also where it sourced those assets from. The source of energy and the use of energy. What we haven't done is look at how every financial event that happens in a business is recorded on the butterfly.

The duality, as shown by the two wings of the butterfly, means that when any event affects the butterfly, two impacts must be recorded, not just one. This way, the butterfly stays in balance. If just one impact was recorded, the total amount on one wing would be higher than the other.

In traditional accounting terms, this is called double-entry bookkeeping. Here are some examples of transactions, each of which causes two impacts:

1. When a business borrows money:
   Impact 1:   It gets cash on the left-hand wing.
   Impact 2:   It makes a promise and gets an obligation on the right-hand wing.

2. When a business pays cash for a table:
   Impact 1:   It loses cash, reducing the assets on the left-hand-side.
   Impact 2:   It gains a table, increasing the assets on the left-hand-side.
               No net effect so both sides stay the same.

3. When a business pays a deposit:
   Impact 1:   It loses a cash asset on the left-hand-side.
   Impact 2:   It gains a deposit asset on the left-hand-side.
               No net effect on the left-hand-side.

4. When a business gets paid up front for two months of coaching not yet delivered:
   Impact 1:   It gets cash, increasing the left-hand side.
   Impact 2:   It records a promise obligation to the client on the right-hand side.

5. When a business gets paid after giving advice (earning revenue):

   Impact 1: It gains cash on the left-hand side.

   Impact 2: It increases the promise to owners on the right-hand side.

The purpose of a business: Owing the owners more

Of the five events that we recorded above, the only one that directly benefited the owners of the business (by increasing the equity promise to them) is number five. Let's take a closer look at that.

We'll assume that the business balance sheet starts out like this, with $50,000 of assets, liabilities of $30,000 and equity of $20,000.

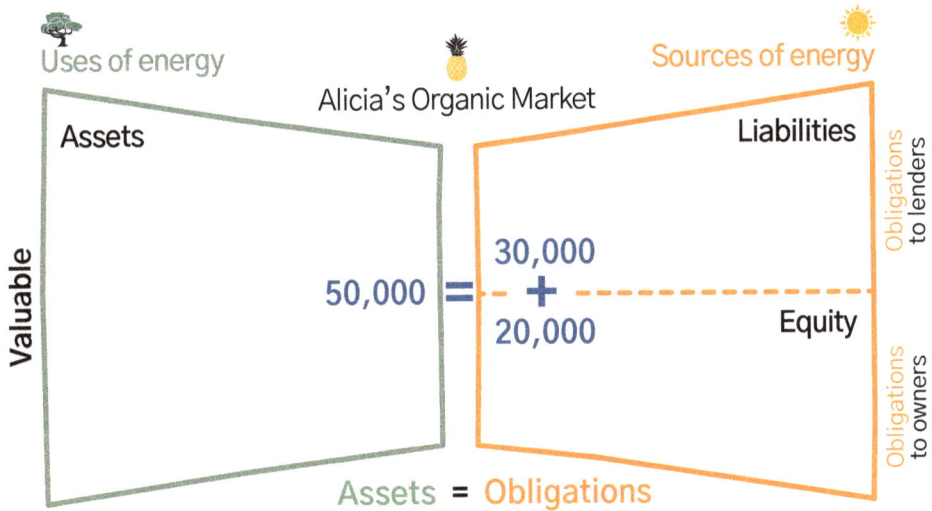

Alicia is multi-talented. As well as selling fruit and vegetables, she uses her master's degree in agriculture to advise local growers on their farming practices. She does that, and one of them pays her for a day of consultation. She gets a net $2,000 for the work.

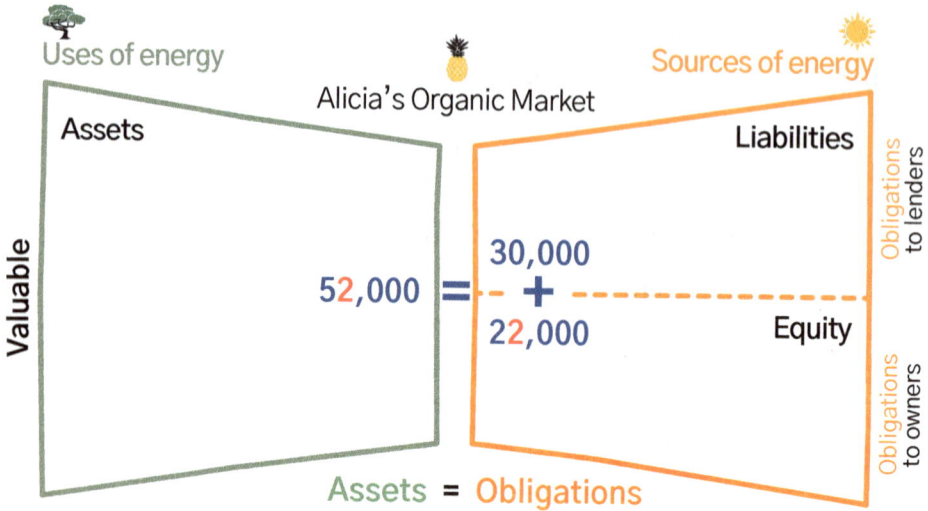

The assets of the business go up from $50,000 to $52,000. What happens on the promises side of the butterfly? Does the business owe the bank more or owe the owner more? Definitely not the bank. They will get their interest when it's due. It's the owner that benefits from the consulting work that Alicia did for the business. The equity increases from $20,000 to $22,000.

Seeing the butterfly in action

Do you feel the power of this dual perspective? We use the butterfly as a visual metaphor for the balance sheet to illustrate this duality:

- One wing shows the sources of funding.
- The other wing shows how that funding has been put to work.

This concept is vital. Much of the confusion in financial conversations happens when one person talks about one wing, and the other talks about the other wing. But both wings are always in play. Always.

The balance sheet in living color

If you've been following along using your own accounting software, like Quick-Books, you will have seen balance sheets formatted differently, stripped of color and conversation, laid out vertically.

That's why we use visuals, metaphors, and most importantly, language, to bring it back to life. The traditional balance sheet layout remains valid, but without context, it can feel cold, confusing, or even intimidating. That's why we created tools like the butterfly and the BaSIS Board to reconnect the data to meaning. You'll learn about the BaSIS Board in the next few pages.

Let's take another look at the standard balance sheet layout for Alicia's Organic Market. This time, we'll fast-forward to when the business has bigger numbers with more account names.

Alicia's Organic Market balance sheet (horizontal with color)

Balance sheet of:

Uses of energy		Alicia's Organic Market	Sources of energy	
ASSETS			**LIABILITIES**	
Current assets			*Current liabilities*	
Cash & deposits	46,000		Borrowings	64,000
Accounts receivable	128,000		Payables	182,000
Inventories	239,000		Total current liabilities	246,000
Total current assets	413,000			
			Non-current liabilities	
Non-current assets			Borrowings	548,000
Land & buildings	502,000		Provisions	30,000
Equipment, fixtures & fittings	177,000		Total non-current liabilities	578,000
Investments in other companies	1,000			
Total non-current assets	680,000		**TOTAL LIABILITIES**	824,000
TOTAL ASSETS	1,093,000		**EQUITY**	
			Issued capital	192,000
			Retained earnings	77,000
			TOTAL EQUITY	269,000

It might appear overwhelming at first with tables, figures, and terms like "total liabilities and equity." But now you know what these terms mean in real life. You understand that behind every number lies a decision, a relationship, and a promise.

- The top portion of the green section shows *cash* for Alicia's Organic Market ($46,000), *receivables*, and *inventory*—those are *current assets*, value that's ready to be used or turned into cash.
- The section below it reflects *buildings*, *equipment*, and *investments*—*non-current (or long-term) assets* ($680,000).
- And on the other side, the orange section represents *liabilities*—borrowings, payables, and provisions.
- The second orange section is where Alicia's relationship to her business lives. This is *equity*. Her investment. Her *retained earnings*. Her return. What the business owes her, because of what she put in, and what the business earned for her.

Suddenly, what once looked like a wall of numbers now tells a story. Even in a more traditional layout—like you'd see in QuickBooks—the butterfly holds true. The wings might be stacked vertically instead of spread horizontally, but the principle remains the same.

Let's look at Alicia's Organic Market again, using a more traditional, vertical layout.

Balance sheet: Traditional vertical layout (colored)

Alicia's Organic Market
Balance sheet as of this year

ASSETS		
Current assets		
Cash & deposits	46,000	*4
Accounts receivable	128,000	
Inventories	239,000	
Total current assets	413,000	
Non-current assets		
Land & buildings	502,000	
Equipment, fixtures & fittings	177,000	
Investments in other companies	1,000	
Total non-current assets	680,000	
TOTAL ASSETS	**1,093,000**	
LIABILITIES		
Current liabilities		
Borrowings	64,000	
Payables	182,000	
Total current liabilities	246,000	
Non-current liabilities		
Borrowings	548,000	
Provisions	30,000	
Total non-current liabilities	578,000	
TOTAL LIABILITIES	**824,000**	
EQUITY		
Issued capital	192,000	*2
Retained earnings	77,000	*3
TOTAL EQUITY	**269,000**	*1

Why does the business owe the owner $269,000 (*1)? Look just above, and you'll see *issued capital* of $192,000 (*2). That's a promise to return the money the owner contributed. The business made a promise to the owner, in the form of *equity*, when the owner put money into the business. It's not "just numbers," it's a representation of your relationship with your business. *Issued capital* doesn't sound like a promise, but it is.

The other $77,000 (*3)? That's retained earnings—the accumulated profits the business has generated. This forms part of the company's promise to the owner and stockholders. Remember, **equity is not money**. It's a promise to give back the money, to work for the owner, to grow their investment and pay them dividends. If you go up to the green section, that's where the money is, called cash and deposits of $46,000 (*4). That, together with all the other current and non-current assets, is what's being promised to owners and other funders, such as the bank lender. Now you can see the balance sheet that's not scary in black and white.

Peter video

Balance sheet: Traditional vertical layout (black and white)

Alicia's Organic Market
Balance sheet as of this year

ASSETS

Current assets

Cash & deposits	46,000
Accounts receivable	128,000
Inventories	239,000
Total current assets	413,000

Non-current assets

Land & buildings	502,000
Equipment, fixtures & fittings	177,000
Investments in other companies	1,000
Total non-current assets	680,000
TOTAL ASSETS	**1,093,000**

LIABILITIES

Current liabilities

Borrowings	64,000
Payables	182,000
Total current liabilities	246,000

Non-current liabilities

Borrowings	548,000
Provisions	30,000
Total non-current liabilities	578,000
TOTAL LIABILITIES	**824,000**

EQUITY

Issued capital	192,000
Retained earnings	77,000
TOTAL EQUITY	**269,000**

5

The income statement and BaSIS Board

In chapter 4, you explored the limiting conversations that shape your financial mindset and you learned about the butterfly balance sheet—how every transaction has two impacts. Now, we'll dive deeper into how your business creates value through the income statement and discover the BaSIS Board—a conversational tool that brings your financial understanding into sharper focus.

By the end of this chapter, you will understand the purpose of the income statement and gain clarity on the remaining two of the five fundamental elements of finance that we call RELAX:

- **R**evenue
- **E**quity
- **L**iabilities
- **A**ssets
- e**X**penses

These five elements work together to form what we call the value cycle. And yes, we invite you to relax into this learning. When you see how each of these elements interconnects, you'll begin to see your business not just as a stream of numbers, but as a living, evolving system of value exchange.

If you created your own balance sheet as part of the action step in the last chapter, how did it feel? Did it confront you a little? That's exactly the point. The exercise helps you see your business with new eyes, objectively. At its core, the balance sheet simply shows what you have and what you've promised.

But to really understand your business, we need to move beyond the idea of just "money in and money out." That perspective can mislead. In this chapter, you'll explore the deeper distinction between value generation and value consumption—a much more meaningful lens through which to understand your business.

And this is where we bring in the BaSIS Board—the heart of our framework. The BaSIS Board brings together everything we've discussed, the butterfly balance sheet from chapter 5 and the five RELAX elements that form your business's communication model.

What makes our program different is that we don't start with formulas or spreadsheets. We start with words, with relationships, with conversations. Yes, there will be numbers, but the real transformation comes when you shift your thinking from "tracking money" to "understanding value."

This is how you begin to see your finances as a value cycle, not just a financial report. Revenue generates value, expenses consume value, assets grow, equity builds, liabilities amplify the process, and the cycle continues. Understanding the BaSIS Board gives you the language and awareness to step confidently into your role as a financially grounded business owner.

It's not about the math, it's about meaning

One of the biggest myths in small business finance is that you need to be good at math to manage your money well. You don't. What you need is a grounding in meaning. And meaning comes from language—from learning to talk about your business in terms of value, movement, and promise.

The BaSIS Board is not just an accounting framework; it's a way to shift how you relate to your business. When you can name each of the RELAX elements, locate them on your financial reports, and understand how they interact, you begin to see your business as an integrated system. They're not just a collection of transactions, but a living cycle of value creation.

That's the power of perspective. And from here, the journey continues.

Let's explore how Alicia's Organic Market illustrates this story and how a business's activities lead to value growth.

Unpacking the profit that's shown in equity

Let's remember from the previous chapter how Alicia's Organic Market began with two sources of funding:

- A loan: $30,000 (liabilities)
- Alicia's personal investment: $20,000 (equity)

And those two obligations funded:

- Total assets = $50,000

This was reflected in the accounting equation:

$$\text{ASSETS} = \text{LIABILITIES} + \text{EQUITY}$$
$$\$50,000 = \$30,000 + \$20,000$$

Alicia's Organic Market then provided some consulting services to a local grower who paid $2,000 cash for those services.

This meant that the assets of the business grew from $50,000 to $52,000. Remember that all the assets of the business must be promised to the funders (lenders and owners) which makes sure that the butterfly stays in balance.

The question then was, which promise increases? The promise to the lenders or the promise to the owners? We saw it's the owners who benefit, so the sources side of the butterfly changed to:

- Liabilities (the bank loan) stays at $30,000
- Equity increases from $20,000 to $22,000

That $2,000 growth in equity is the profit. **Profit = the growth in the prom-**

ise to the owner. Profit isn't an asset. It's not the $2,000 in the asset box, it's the increase in what the business owes Alicia.

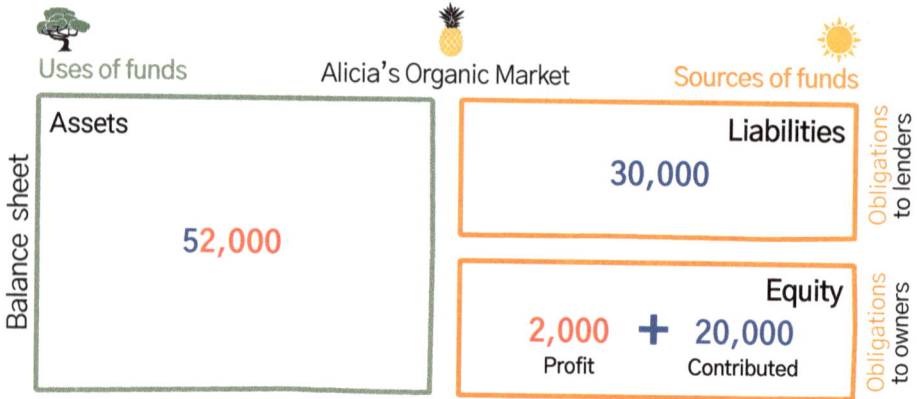

Alicia's Organic Market

Uses of funds — Sources of funds

Balance sheet

Assets

52,000

Liabilities

30,000

Obligations to lenders

Equity

2,000 + **20,000**

Profit — Contributed

Obligations to owners

Now consider that the additional $2,000 profit in the equity was actually the net profit after the business incurred travel expenses to get Alicia to the client. But what were the gross amounts that netted to the $2,000?

- Scenario A: Did the business gain $3,000 and lose $1,000, leaving $2,000 profit?, or
- Scenario B: Did the business gain $100,000 and lose $98,000, also leaving $2,000 profit?

The difference between how much value you generate and how much you sacrifice is your margin. Smaller losses to earn a given profit mean better margins and a more efficient business.

The profit margin in scenario A is 66%, because $2,000 is 60% of $3,000. The profit margin in scenario B is 2%, because $2,000 is 2% of $100,000.

Profit margins are important for a business owner to track and manage. So, the accounting system needs a way to report the gross numbers that give the net profit in the equity section. And that is what the income statement is for.

BaSIS Board

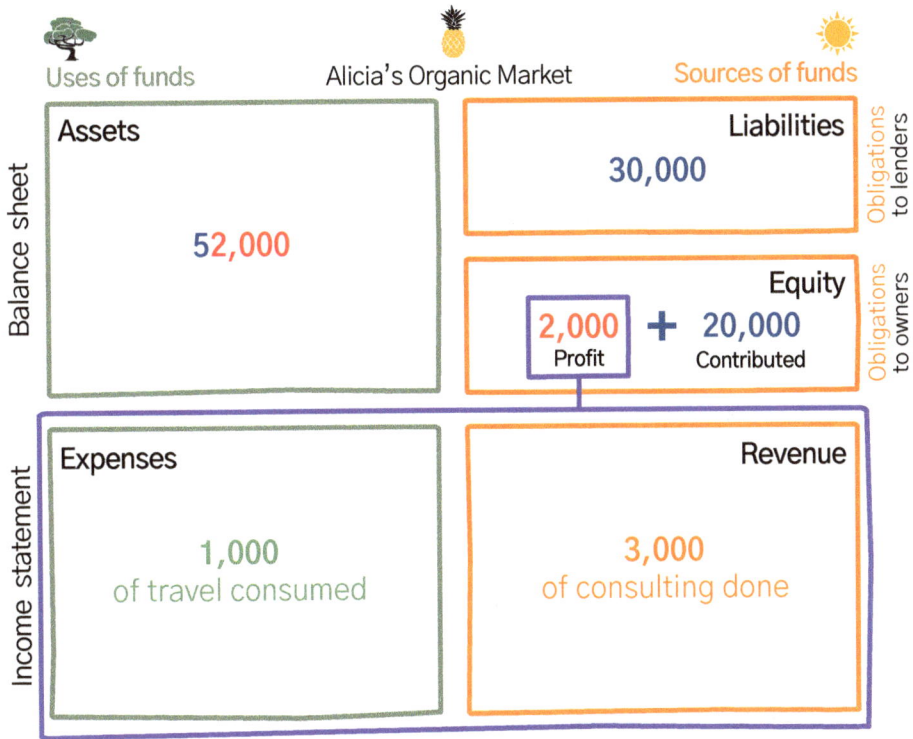

The diagram above shows the BaSIS Board. The name comes from **Ba**lance **S**heet plus **I**ncome **S**tatement. The top three boxes are the balance sheet, the same butterfly we've been using. And the bottom two boxes form the income statement, which now explains how the profit in the equity section was generated.

In our organic market scenario, the profit of $2,000 was generated by doing consulting worth $3,000 and incurring expenses of $1,000.

And that is what the BaSIS Board now shows us. In the bottom-right orange box, we see the third source of energy to the business—the best source!—which is revenue. And in the bottom-left green box, we see the second use of energy, which is expenses.

CASE STUDY:

Understanding the income statement in action

Consider Sarah, a consultant who struggled to understand why her bank balance didn't match her "profit." She had $15,000 in her business account, but her bookkeeper said she made $25,000 profit last quarter. The confusion cleared when she learned:

- She had earned $45,000 in revenue ($35,000 paid as cash and $10,000 still owed by clients).
- She had incurred $20,000 in expenses ($15,000 paid and $5,000 owing on her credit card).
- Her profit was, indeed, $25,000, but cash and profit are different things.
- The income statement showed her business performance, while the bank showed just one asset.

This revelation transformed how Sarah made decisions. She stopped checking her bank balance before making investments and started looking at her complete financial picture.

Beware: Revenue and expenses are widely misunderstood

You've now met the BaSIS Board, a powerful and holistic lens through which you can see the finances of your business. This visual representation of the communication model of accounting supports the communication models of finance and business too.

The BaSIS Board:

- Has three sources of energy, shown in orange: Liabilities, equity, and revenue
- Has two uses of energy, shown in green: Assets and expenses

- Represents the traditional balance sheet and income statement reports
- Indicates how the bottom two income statement boxes explain how profit increased equity (or possibly how a loss reduced the equity)

You're clear about the nature of assets, which are valuable. And you know that liabilities and equity are promises—obligations to creditors and owners respectively. And the financial purpose of the business is to grow its obligation to its owner.

What we need to get very clear on now is the definition—the nature of revenue and expenses. They are not cash coming in and cash going out, as people casually think. In the communication model of accounting, revenue and expenses are specialized terms that describe the activities of the business.

Revenue

Revenue is activity that increases profit by increasing assets (or alternatively decreasing liabilities). Value-generating activity.

Expenses

Expenses are activity that decreases profit by consuming or sacrificing assets (or alternatively increasing liabilities). Value-sacrificing activity.

Being clear on these definitions is very important. They explain why profit and cash received are not the same thing.

Revenue is not cash flow

In the case study example about Sarah, the consultant who struggled to understand why her bank balance didn't match her profit, Sarah confused revenue with cash received. She completed $45,000 of work and correctly reported that amount of revenue. But we know that $10,000 of that amount is still owed to Sarah. Which means she had only received $35,000 cash up to that point. You can earn a profit while receiving no cash.

Revenue is value-generating activity, not only cash-generating activity. The value can be in any form. In the scenario with Sarah, the value-generating activity that she performed manifested as $35,000 of cash and $10,000 of account receivable. Remember, being owed money is great, it's valuable. Even if it's not quite as good as having cash.

BaSIS Board with definitions

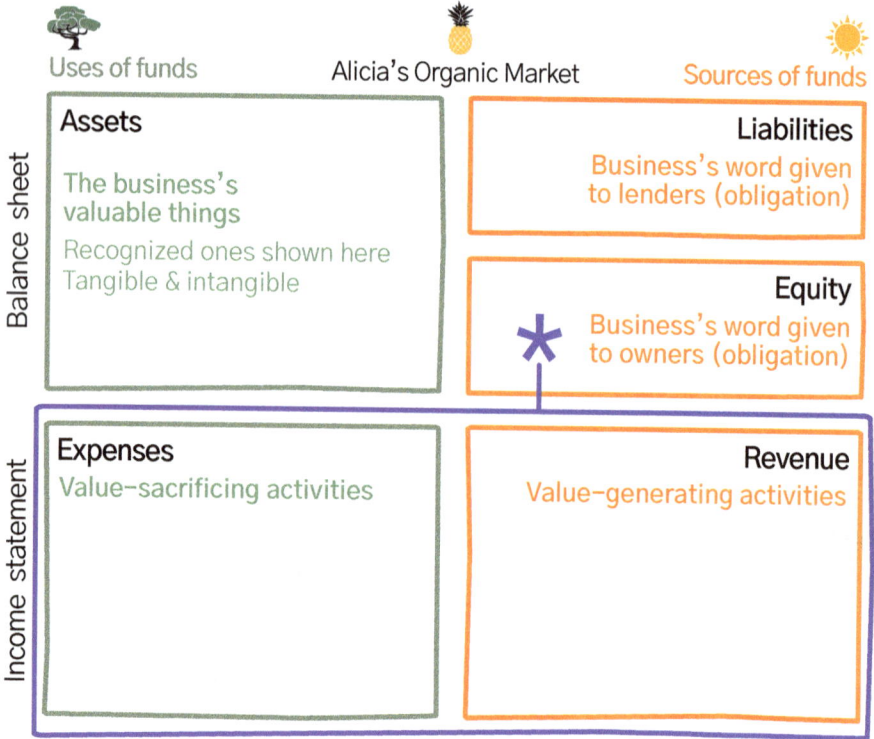

The income statement is referred to by many names, including profit and loss statement, P&L, statement of financial performance, statement of operations, and statement of activities. This reminds us that it describes performance and activities. You can think of revenue as a verb, an action word. It's what the business does to make assets grow.

- Revenue → Value-generating activity (e.g., advising clients, selling products)
- Expenses → Value-sacrificing activity (e.g., employees clocking their hours, using up inventory)

Revenue, in this instance, is used as a verb, not a noun. It's the action that creates value. Cash may not have come in yet, but the right to receive it has been created.

You may feel accomplished at the end of a workday, even without getting paid. That's because you've created revenue—value-generating activity. You've earned the right to be paid.

Here's a "sale of goods" example:

- A business buys a chair from a vendor for $400, which it records as an inventory asset
- It sells the chair for $1,000
- It gains $1,000 (cash or receivables)
- It sacrifices $400 (inventory)

The sale event results in a net gain in assets of $600. And the profit within equity attributes those additional assets to the owners. The $600 profit is not cash. It's the growth in the promise the business owes its owner.

RELAX: The five accounting elements

The five elements that you see on the BaSIS Board or on a traditional balance sheet represent the basis of business accounting, so it's important to have a clear understanding of them:

1. **Assets** (noun, valuable things, what the business controls)
2. **Liabilities** (noun, the obligation to non-owners to return assets or provide services to them)
3. **Equity** (noun, the obligation to the owners, attributing residual assets to them)
4. **Revenue** (verb, value-generating activity)
5. **Expenses** (verb, value-sacrificing activity)

Let's remember that not all activity has a measurable value. As a business owner, you might:

- Give free talks
- Build your reputation

- Grow unrecognized assets

Eventually the unrecognized assets like goodwill will hopefully generate sales and cash.

Negative equity

It's also possible for a business to have negative equity. Consider that a business has:

- Assets = $300,000
- Liabilities = $1,000,000
- Equity = -$700,000

In this scenario, the business owes more to creditors than it owns. That's negative equity. There's not enough value for the owner and to fully repay the creditors. Since the equity figure is negative, it should mean that instead of the business owing the shareholders, the shareholders should owe the business and be required to put more money in. But that's what the "limited" in "limited liability corporation" means.

It means that the responsibility of the shareholders is limited to what they've already put in, and they can't be required to pay more into the company to cover its debts.

Leverage

When a business borrows money from creditors, it can increase the company's return on equity. Borrowing is called leverage because it multiplies the earnings. Because the borrowed assets are put to work and generate more than the cost of borrowing, the surplus earnings that the borrowed assets generated are attributed to the shareholders. So they earn from the assets they contributed as well as from the assets others contributed.

It's a way to amplify the business's financial capacity and pursue growth beyond what its current resources would allow. Let's consider this further with an example from our fictional business:

Alicia's Organic Market has:

- Assets: $50,000
- Debt: $30,000
- **Leverage = 60%**

Some debt proves healthy; it allows you to gain more assets and grow faster. Too little debt can be a missed opportunity. Public companies with low debt are at risk of being taken over.

Balance sheet versus income statement

The balance sheet represents where a business is "at"—a snapshot in time. The income statement tells the story of how it got there and how it's doing in terms of generating and sacrificing value.

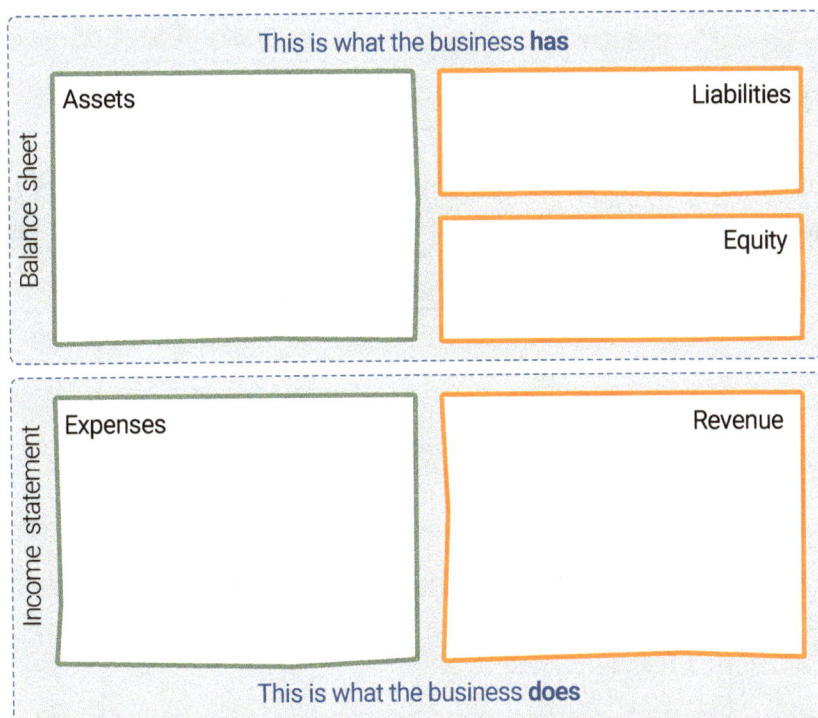

61

Traditional income statement

A traditional income statement is typically laid out as follows, shown here with arbitrary numbers. The revenue is shown at the top, and then the expenses are chunked into categories: direct, operating, and tax. A subtotal is calculated under each type.

Traditional income statement

Sales	1,000
Cost of sales expenses	250
Gross profit	750
Operating expenses	50
Operating profit	700
Tax expense	150
Profit after tax	550

ACTION STEPS

1. Draw up an income statement for your business, and draw the BaSIS Board by hand like this:

Assets Business's valuable things	Liabilities Promises to lenders
	Equity Promises to owners
eXpenses Activities that sacrifice value	Revenue Activities that generate value

2. Explain what the acronym RELAX means to a friend.

3. Think about the value cycle of your business. What value does your business generate? What value does it sacrifice? How efficiently does it convert one to the other?

4. Answer these ten key questions for analyzing your balance sheet:

    1) What's the current ratio (current assets/current liabilities), and how has it changed over time?

    2) How much debt is the company carrying relative to equity, and what portion is short-term versus long-term?

    3) What's the composition of accounts receivable, and has the collection period increased or decreased?

    4) Are inventory levels appropriate for the business model, and how has inventory turnover changed?

    5) What's the quality of the assets? Are they working hard to generate revenue and profit?

    6) How much cash does the company maintain relative to its operational needs?

    7) Are there any significant off-balance sheet liabilities or contingent obligations that need to be recorded, possibly in the notes to the financial reports instead of the balance sheet itself?

    8) What's the working capital trend, and does it support the company's growth plans? Working capital is the funding to cover day-to-day operational assets like accounts receivable and inventory.

    9) What's the composition and quality of shareholders' equity (common stock, preferred stock, additional paid-in capital)?

    10) Is there material goodwill on the balance sheet, and if so, has it been tested for impairment recently?

The habit of seeing and thinking double

Now we want to continue building your skills and confidence to better take control of the future of your business. One of the ways we do this is by getting you to practice "thinking double." We playfully call it **"pow-pow" thinking**.

The BaSIS Board is a communication model that gives you a whole-story view of your business's finances. To benefit from the power of the framework to support your decisions and commitments, it works to appreciate how all the accounts and numbers get onto the framework. In other words, to understand the framework's logic.

Underpinning the logic of the BaSIS Board is double-entry accounting. All that means is whenever anything happens in your business—when a financial transaction takes place—the framework is impacted in not one way, but two. When you understand the two impacts of any transaction, you can more readily follow any financial conversation and engage more effectively, making more informed decisions with your financial, operational, and advisory support teams. You become more powerful as a business owner.

So we'll explore a few typical business transactions below using *pow-pow* thinking. It brings to life the balance sheet butterfly—assets on one side, liabilities and equity on the other. And within equity, we'll track the profit that's growing it, explained by revenue and expenses as revealed in the income statement. It's more than bookkeeping. *Pow-pow* thinking is a way to see the full story.

Let's break it down through examples.

EARN AND GET PAID (POW–POW):

The market makes a sale and gets paid cash.

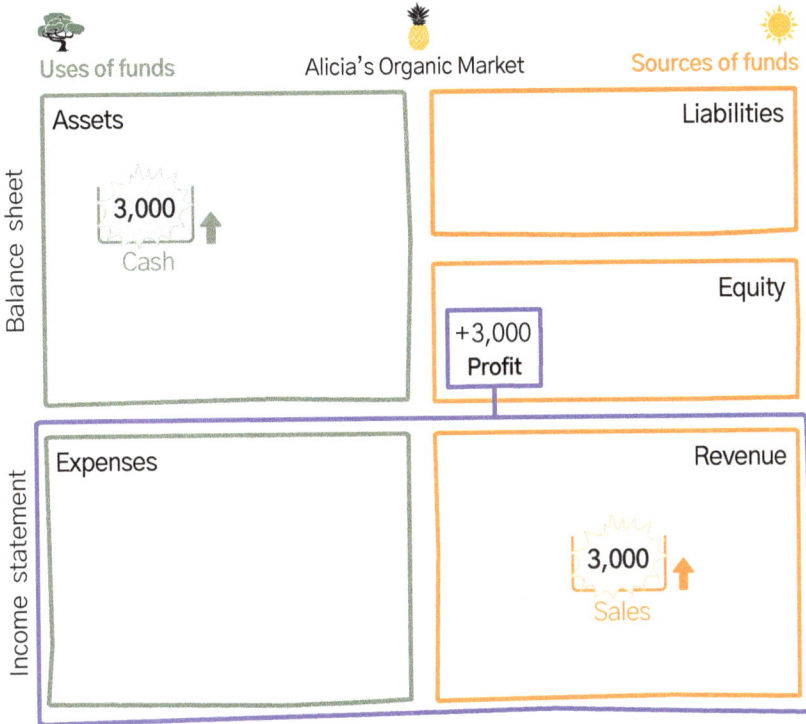

The business makes a sale, which is revenue. That's the activity, the sound of which could be "Thank you for your business, it's been a pleasure serving you." And the result of the activity is cash coming in, the sound is "ka-ching" as the cash register opens. That's your first *pow-pow*—your business made a sale and got cash. It increases both your income and your assets. This is the "double entry" of double entry accounting, and you'll see how the purple box within equity is profit.

Whenever anything happens in sales or expenses below, profit in equity changes. That's automatic, because sales and expenses roll up into profit. This scenario is the simplest and most critical business transaction. Do work or sell (verb) something; get paid something (noun) for it.

EARN NOW, GET PAID LATER (POW-POW):

Sell on credit.

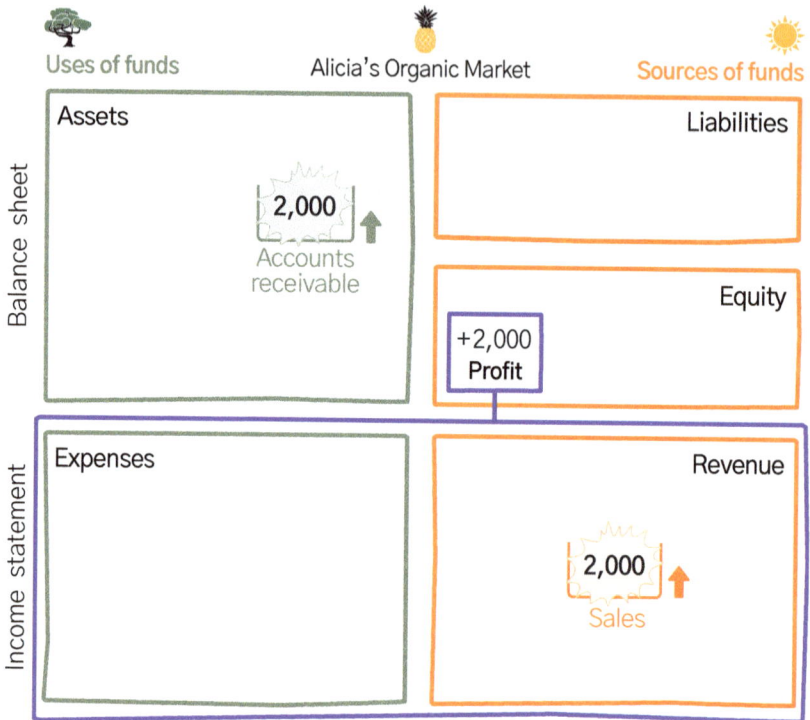

You perform a service today and invoice the client. That's revenue and accounts receivable. You're owed the money, and your books reflect the value you've created. On the BaSIS Board above, your work—the sale—is the bottom right hand corner of $2,000. Now you're owed $2,000. It's valuable. It's an asset, and you'll eventually turn that asset into cash. Remember, you recognize a sale even if you haven't yet been paid, because you've generated something valuable, in this case the right to be paid.

GET PAID FIRST, DELIVER LATER (POW-POW):

Sometimes you're in the fortunate position of getting paid before you have delivered the service to your client. Imagine a client buys a gift card for $150 from you.

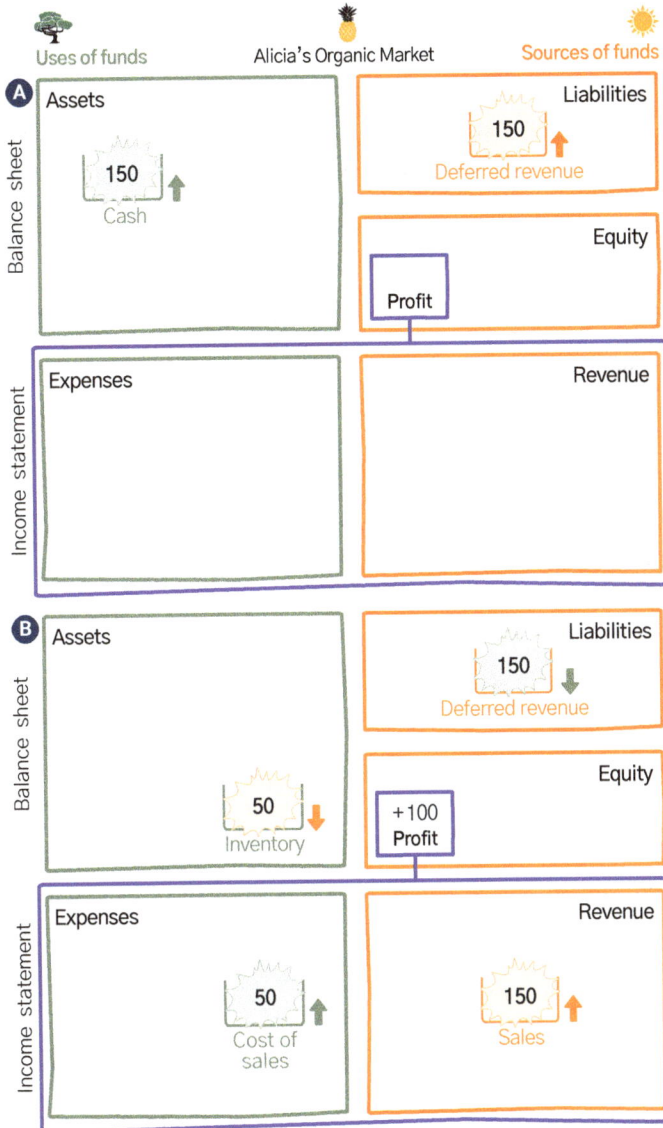

You receive money up front but haven't delivered the service yet. That's not revenue—it's a liability because you owe the work. It shows up as deferred revenue until you deliver. On the BaSIS Board above (A), the cash goes up in assets when the customer buys the gift card. And at the same time, the liability account, called deferred revenue, goes up. (It sounds like a revenue account, but it's not! Accounting terminology is often like that.) There's no profit impact yet, because nothing happened in the income statement. Later (B), when you provide the service to the client or sell them an item, the revenue is recognized. That means that the liability (deferred revenue) goes down, and the revenue (sales) goes up together with profit. Inventory decreases because the business gave some to the customer. Giving away inventory is a value-sacrificing activity, so cost of sales increase.

INCUR EXPENSE AND PAY (POW–POW):

Imagine you incur an expense and pay for it immediately. Remember, an expense is a value-consuming activity. Maybe the expense is travel or taking a client out for a meal.

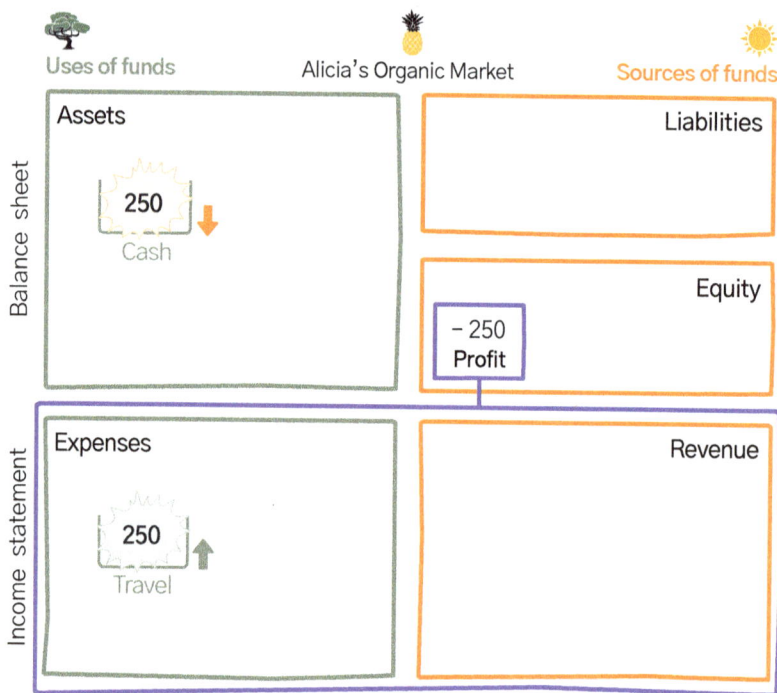

You incur expenses and pay. The traveling or eating is an expense. And the cash goes out because of the expense. *Pow-pow.* Of course, profit goes down automatically. You can think of it as the same second *pow*: the travel and the profit reduction have the same effect. The top three boxes must balance on their own because they form the butterfly. The left wing goes down because of the cash, and the right wing decreases because of the profit. The bottom two boxes of the BaSIS Board are the income statement. They provide the detail of the change in profit. If you think of the whole green side of the BaSIS Board, the *uses* side, it stays in balance because assets went up and expenses went down. So no overall change on the green side. When you're adding all the orange boxes on the *sources* side, you don't count the purple number in profit. So there's no change on the right hand side of the overall BaSIS Board.

INCUR EXPENSE, PAY LATER (POW-POW):

Let's say you purchase special software or a subscription for your company. You incur the expense now but pay later (perhaps on a credit card). There's the software expense of $500. And now you owe the credit card company. But immediately there's the $500 reduction in profit (purple box).

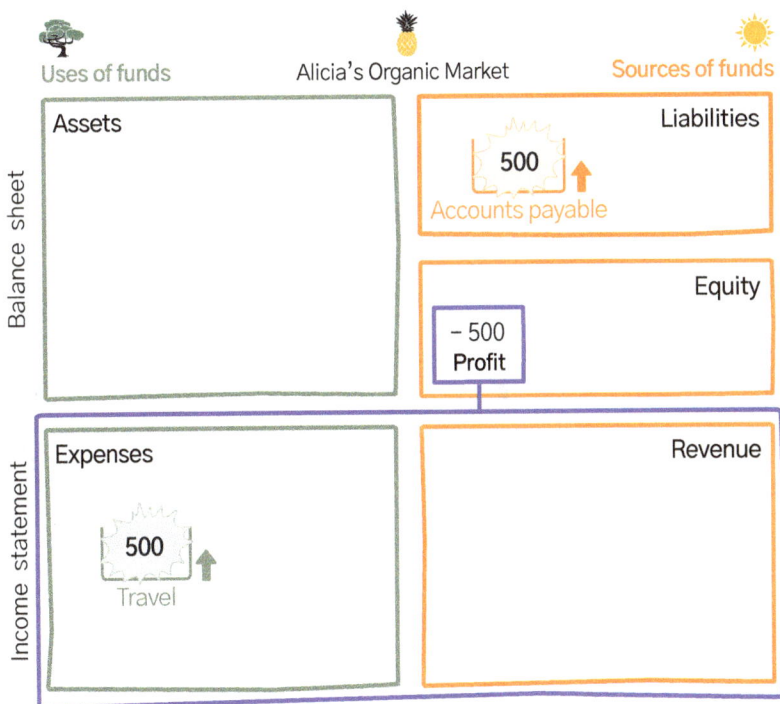

Did you notice the green and orange arrows next to the accounts? They represent traditional debiting and crediting. Green is debiting; orange is crediting. Green arrows cause increases on the green side of the BaSIS Board and decreases on the orange side. Orange decreases the green side and increases the orange side.

CASE STUDY:

Pow-pow in practice

Mark, an attorney, couldn't understand why his cash flow was tight despite being busy. *Pow-pow* thinking revealed the issue:

- He billed clients $50,000 (revenue up, receivables up: *pow-pow*).
- He paid contractor attorneys $30,000 (expenses up, cash down: *pow-pow*).
- His profit showed $20,000, but his cash was negative $30,000.

The revelation? He was financing his clients' legal work. By implementing retainers (cash up, deferred revenue up) and progress billing, he transformed his cash flow while maintaining the same profit levels.

ACTION STEPS

Begin to observe and write your daily business events in *pow-pow* terms.

- What was the value generated?
- What was the value consumed?
- How did it affect the RELAX elements on the BaSIS Board?

Peter video

TESTIMONIAL

> **"**
>
> *This course surpassed my expectations. Being able to understand the records I'm holding and allocating them in the correct RELAX format has made a huge difference. I think many women really don't understand finance, and if they attended this it would help break this barrier.* - Neha G., Housing Developer

6

RELAX, it's about the system

By now you know that RELAX is our acronym for the five elements of financial reporting:

- **R**evenue: Value-generating activity
- **E**quity: The owner's stake in the business
- **L**iabilities: What the business owes others
- **A**ssets: What the business owns or is owed
- e**X**penses: Value-sacrificing activity

RELAX and the BaSIS Board conversational framework is not just a teaching tool. It provides a complete framework for seeing the flow of value through your business.

Peter often says, "There are only two things happening in your business at any given moment: you are either generating value, or you are consuming it."

You don't need a finance degree to track this. You only need the courage to look and engage with your business as the separate entity that it is.

The assets, liabilities and equity are what the business system is using to generate value. And the income statement gives the detail of what it did with those resources to generate value.

The income statement: Value in motion

	Income statement Jan – Mar	
	Retail business	Consulting business
Revenue		
Sale of goods	240,000	120,000
Less: Direct expenses		
Inventory provided to customers/Other sales expense	80,000	5,000
Gross profit	**160,000**	**115,000**
Less: Indirect expenses		
Salaries	76,000	60,000
Rent	40,000	2,000
Utilities	14,000	2,000
Advertising and marketing	10,000	6,000
Other	5,000	5,000
Total expenses	145,000	75,000
Operating profit	**15,000**	**40,000**
Tax expense		
Tax	3,000	10,000
Profit after tax	**12,000**	**30,000**

Let's tell the stories of the two businesses described in the income statement above: one, a retail business, and the other, a consulting business. Their profit margins are different, reflecting the typical cost structures of each industry.

The retail narrative reads something like this: In the quarter through March, the business sold $240,000 worth of goods, which inventory had cost the business $80,000 to acquire. The gross profit on those sales was $160,000, a 66% gross margin. The business sacrificed $145,000 worth of value as operating expenses, the biggest of which were salaries and rent, resulting in an operating profit of $15,000. The tax sacrifice was $3,000, resulting in a profit after tax for the quarter of $12,000. This represents a 5% net profit margin, which is fairly typical for a retail business.

The consulting narrative might read like this: The consultancy provided $120,000 worth of advice, incurring $5,000 of expenses to deliver those services, such as travel to the client. The gross profit was $115,000. The consultants were paid a salary of $60,000 during the period—by far the largest expense. The value sacrificed to operate the business amounted to $75,000. This left an operating profit of $40,000 and an after-tax profit of $30,000. This represents a 25% profit margin, in line with the industry average for a consulting business.

The relaxed conversational tone of these narratives is deliberate. What we're encouraging you to do is have your own continual—even if unspoken and subconscious—ever-present narrative like these for your own business.

In one of our workshops, a participant shared that she noticed what she thought was a loss in January because of a large service charge. But realizing that the expense covered twelve months, not just the month it was paid, she saw the business was profitable overall. That kind of insight transforms the way you lead.

You'll adapt the narrative to your own circumstances, bringing new insights to how you are running your business. One coach described her limited client capacity as "inventory." But she later realized, "It's not physical inventory – but it is finite. My time is my product."

Whether you sell therapy services or handcrafted goods, your income statement reflects the same value generation and sacrifices activities within your business's RELAX value cycle.

CASE STUDY:

The service business reality

A therapist we've worked with became more conscious of the limited amount of time she had each month. She realized that she could do much better if she reworked her main offering. She had been charging $500 for five individual sessions, thinking she made a good profit and rate per hour. But when she thought more holistically, using the RELAX value cycle and with greater awareness of the separateness of the business from herself, she found:

- Revenue: $500
- Hours per package: five
- Hourly rate that she had thought of as final earnings: $100
- Share of secretarial support and rent allocation for five sessions: $150
- Actual net-earnings per hour: $70 ($500–$150 for five hours)

Realizing that her hourly net-earnings were 30% less than she'd been thinking led her to restructure her operations. She raised the package to $750 and focused on group sessions to leverage her time. She made her most popular offering her most profitable one, too.

You get to choose the value cycle narrative

The narratives above focus on the income statement part of the value cycle. The five RELAX elements of the communication model form the basis of the bigger picture narrative that includes your balance sheet as well.

What's important when planning your business's full value cycle narrative is that you decide what the RELAX elements are in service to. In the same way you get to write the story of your life, you give voice to the story of your business.

The narrative might, for example, describe:

- How the business goes about generating a profit for its owners (a profit maximization narrative), or
- The interaction between the five RELAX elements as the business generates a social impact in the environment in which it operates (a social impact or nonprofit narrative)

We'll illustrate these two possible narratives below.

In the next chapter, we'll cover a future-focused story reflecting your business's budgeting and planning.

Profit maximization

Consider that you established your business to make a profit for you and other owners. You establish an intention for the business. That's what the "talking-head" icon in the equity section of the BaSIS Board represents.

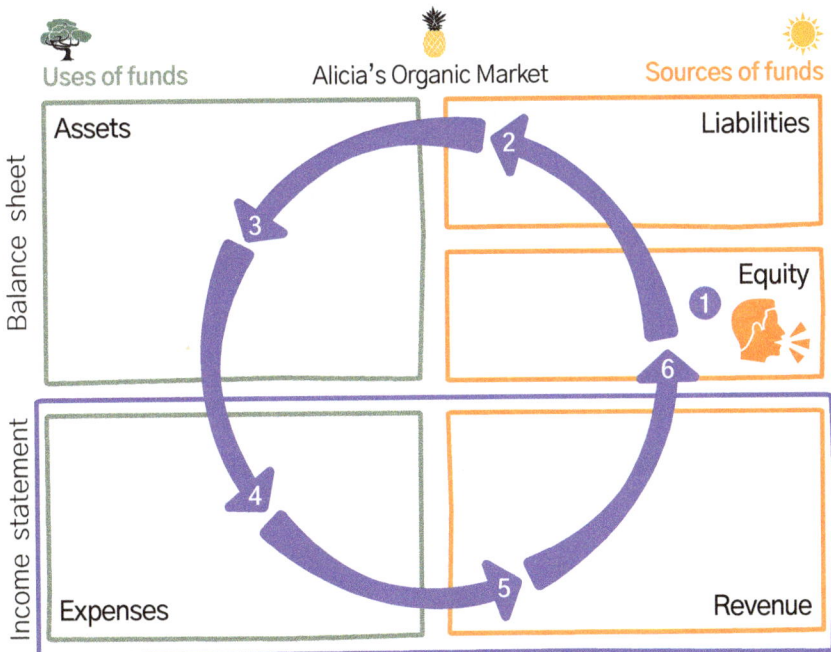

The intention of the business is to grow its promise to its owners. A narrative describing how the business uses its energy and resources to fulfill on that commitment could read as follows:

> The business sourced funding from the owners by making equity promises (1) to those investors. It sources further energy by sourcing additional funding by making liability promises (2) to lenders and creditors. Those two sources of energy enabled the business to acquire valuable assets (3) that the business will use in its operations.

> The business willingly sacrifices some value as expenses (4) with the intention of generating more value than that as revenue (5). The net-value generated is attributed to the shareholders in the form of profit (6), which is the generated promise made to shareholders.

Social impact

Some businesses are established with a different intent than maximizing profit. Their commitment is to make an impact on a particular community. Their purpose may be to positively impact the environment or to feed children in war zones. If you created such a business, your narrative for it could be as follows:

> The intent of the organization is to provide healthcare to underserviced communities (1) in the expense element below. To achieve this intent, the business raises funds through donations and grants and by providing services to clients (2). The assets are held in trust, with a promise that they be used to benefit stakeholders (3). Sometimes, the organization has to owe creditors (4) such as lenders and utility companies, which helps fund the organization's assets (5) and smooth cash flow. The assets are then consumed (6) to create the external impact in the community that has the organization achieve its purpose.

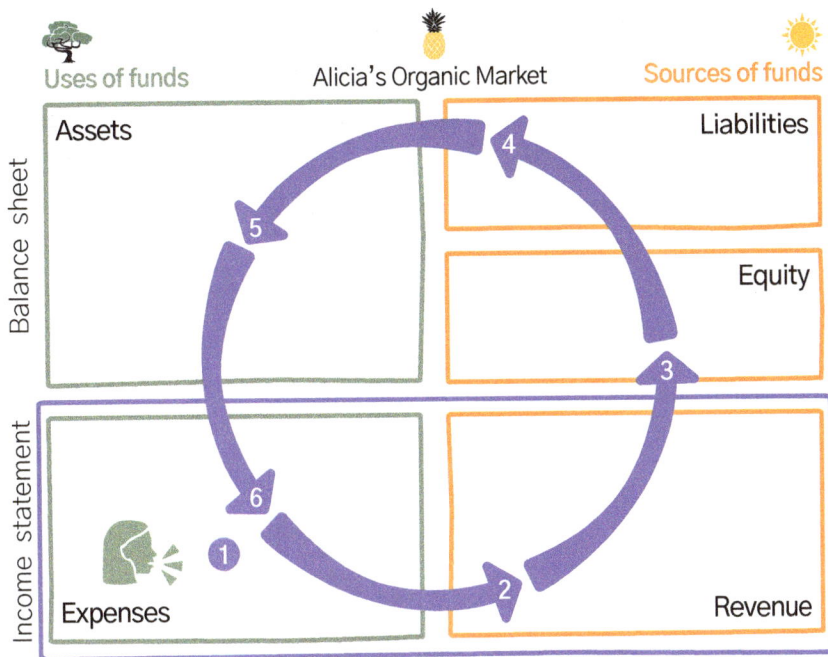

We've seen the two value cycles describing two different types of business, reflecting the intention of each business and the subsequent interplay of the elements of each to achieve its purpose.

Now let's introduce a third value cycle, focused on the future. That, after all, is the main purpose of this book—to have you positioned to design a future of your choosing for you and your business. This third value cycle focuses on the future and reflects your plans, actions, and commitments to realize your business goals.

Planning and budgeting value cycle

The logic of a planning, forecasting, and budgeting value cycle can be expressed to support both a for-profit and a not-for-profit purpose. The future-focused narrative, illustrated on the next page, could read something like this:

The company commits to achieve a certain amount of profit (1) in the upcoming accounting period. To achieve this profit, the business must generate an amount of value (2), which value-generating activity will require a corresponding (and lesser) amount of value-sacrifice (3). To support that level of value-generating and value-sacrificing activities, the business will need a calculated amount of assets (4) such as inventory and fixed assets. Holding that amount of assets may require borrowing from lenders (5), and borrowing will leverage the equity funding (6) that the business uses.

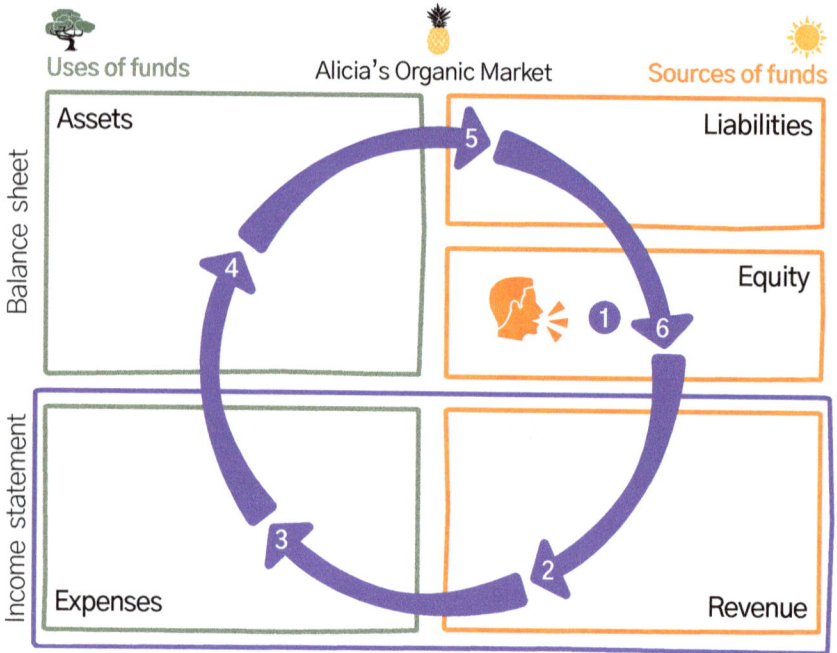

TESTIMONIAL

> "
> *I gained a lot of financial knowledge from this course and would recommend it to small business owners. I gained an understanding of the terminology so I could be 'in the conversation' and understand what is being discussed. I know how to look at a balance sheet/income statement, and can consider how to work on my own business.* - Elly C., Business Owner

7

The bridge to the future

The last chapter looked at three different value cycle narratives. Two were about different business goals: making a profit and making a social impact. The third was about planning for your business's future.

This chapter is about the future and what gets you there. It challenges you to plan the future of your business—consciously, and deliberately—from the communication model of business. This isn't about creating a vision board; it's about committing to a financial future that aligns with your business's core purpose. Your leadership will guide you to that future.

Accounting is an essential tool for your leadership. As Peter puts it, "You're not doing accounting for the IRS - you're doing it for you, driven by your business's purpose. It's your steering wheel."

The mantra of this book has been, *you are not your business.*

As business owners ourselves, we've learned this concept the hard way. For a decade, Kelly collapsed her identity with that of her business. Every challenge, failure, or success felt personal. But once Kelly realized she had collapsed her identity and that she could house her vision inside a separate entity—an asset of value—everything changed. Instead of working solo as an executive leadership coach, she restructured her company to include other talented coaches and expanded the company's reach and prestige. She changed the name of her business from Townsend Consulting Group to Leaders Team.

After discovering the potential for business, Kelly envisioned a significantly broader future for herself and others. Her dedication to impacting leaders was amplified through this business venture, enabling her to offer opportunities for contribution and self-expression to individuals like herself. She could also leave a legacy beyond herself.

Peter also learned the hard way. He used one credit card for his personal expenses and business expenses, making it much harder to split them up later. Bad idea. He also brought a limiting belief about his skills and capability in sales to the business. He knew he had an important idea and product with a special contribution to make, but he let his "block" around sales get in the way of growing the business. Peter gained clarity on the business's purpose, which led to the development of a supportive sales process. We're inviting you to make that same shift. When you recognize your business as something separate from you, you can design, delegate, and commit in an entirely new way.

Peter and Kelly made two powerful commitments for their businesses. The first was a commitment to the purpose of the business. The second was a commitment to a financial target that would be the evidence of the business's success. This next section of the book is about you reflecting and planning from a future-focused value cycle and creating the same kind of clarity for yourself and the people you lead.

The two most important commitments for your business

1. What is your business's purpose? (What does it exist for?)
2. What is its financial growth commitment? (What will its RELAX elements be in three years' time?)

The RELAX framework becomes a tool for designing a system that builds the future value cycle of your business. The diagram on page 81, with its now- and future value cycles shows that the bridge to the future is your leadership and you being accountable for the future value cycle.

Business: Now

Assets	Liabilities
	Equity
Expenses	Revenue

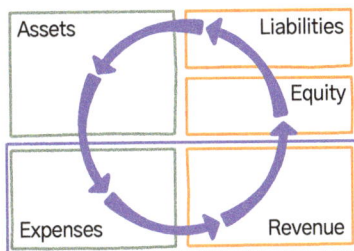

Business: Future

Assets	Liabilities
	Equity
Expenses	Revenue

LEADERSHIP ----▶

-------------▶

ACCOUNTABILITY-▶

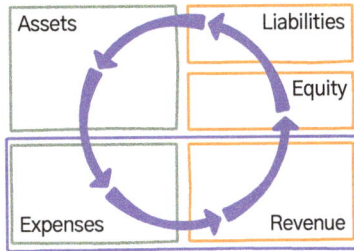

Both of those commitments—purpose and financial growth—are not just positive thinking. The exercise of creating a future value cycle is not pipe dreaming. Purpose and financial growth are critical commitments. The future value cycle is a practical framework for designing the business's future, promoting accountability, and alignment.

Your business's purpose ("Why are we even doing this?")

Committing to a future value cycle supports people working together towards something everyone can align on. We explore the purpose that drives the financial future you are choosing, and we examine the elements of the future value cycle. Together, they form a framework for decision making, using the future value cycle as your map. It's about knowing where you're going and how you're going to get there.

What's the real reason your business exists? Not just what you do, but what difference do you want to make? At Leaders Team, our purpose is to coach and consult business leaders and teams inside our unique transformational methodology, empowering alignment and high performance in a you-and-me business culture. Maybe your purpose is to bring families together, create fun experiences, or simply make people's lives easier. When you know your "why," decisions get easier, and your team gets aligned and inspired. Wealthvox's purpose is to transform financial literacy so that everyone gets that they belong in the financial conversations of their life, at work, and at home.

This isn't just about what you do but what matters. Author and inspirational business speaker, Simon Sinek, has several great TED talks that you can find on YouTube which show how valuable it is to get your "why." He makes the point that people buy from you because they relate to what your company is about and how you do business, not just your product.

Knowing a business's *why* is crucial because it simplifies decision-making, inspires the team, and differentiates the business from competitors. Customers are more likely to align with and be drawn to a business that clearly articulates its purpose.

CASE STUDY:

Purpose drives performance

Angie, a travel advisor, struggled for years to differentiate herself in a crowded market. She competed on price, worked long hours, and felt exhausted. When asked to declare her business's purpose, she initially said, "To book travel." But that wasn't a purpose, it was a function. After deep reflection, she chose: "To create lifetime memories through customized vacations that reconnect families." This commitment, though seemingly insignificant to many, revolutionized everything, imbuing her business with a renewed sense of purpose.

- She stopped competing on price and started charging for her expertise.
- She specialized in multi-generational family trips.
- She created pre-trip planning sessions to understand family dynamics.
- She partnered with destinations that offered meaningful experiences.

Within eighteen months, her average booking value increased by 300%, and she worked with 40% fewer clients while earning twice as much. More importantly, by declaring the purpose of her business, Angie fell in love with her work again. Declaring a purpose didn't just guide her business, it re-energized it.

ACTION STEPS

Take some time to reflect on these questions:

- Why did you start (or join) this business in the first place?
- What problem or need were you most passionate about solving?
- When you first imagined this company, what did you hope it would become?
- How is the world, community, or industry better because your company exists?
- How do you want customers to feel after interacting with your business?
- If your company disappeared tomorrow, what would people miss most?
- What values do you refuse to compromise on—no matter the cost?
- If you could be known for only one thing, what would it be?
- What's a decision you've made in the past that truly reflects what your company stands for?

Even if you have already done this kind of work, it may be time to look again and maybe involve others, such as a coworker or business partner. Is everyone aligned on the purpose? Is the purpose present for people daily? Do you apply the purpose to decision making?

TESTIMONIAL

> **"**
>
> *We are meeting with our accountant next week to start new systems; we are now conducting weekly meetings with partners and biweekly meetings with staff, which will, in turn, force us to start record keeping in a way we had not before. The meetings will hold us accountable. Before this, there was no record keeping.*
>
> - Elena B., Attorney

Defining your future revenue

What do you want your business to look like, numbers-wise, in three years? This isn't just a random goal, it's your promise to yourself and your business. It shapes your hiring, your spending, and even how you talk to customers. Committing to how your revenue, equity, liabilities, assets, and expenses will be in thirty-six months is useful and creates a powerful draw towards that future you are designing.

In practice, it's not a trivial exercise to forecast and plan all five of the RELAX elements that will shape your future value cycle. Typically, developing a strategy and plan that impacts all RELAX elements requires a detailed and thorough exercise, and is something you would do with the support of your financial and leadership coaches. By understanding how value is created and exchanged, you can now effectively participate with financial experts in shaping how your organization will create value in the future.

One of the five RELAX elements has a particularly powerful gravitational pull on all other elements. This is, of course, your future revenue. While we encourage you to keep working with your financial and management team to create a future value cycle with all five elements forecasted, now is a good time to commit to your future revenue.

Do this with a broad brush, for now. The details of what assets, borrowing, etc., that will be needed to achieve the revenue will become clearer later.

Shaping the size and form of your revenue informs your resource planning, funding, staffing, asset allocation, marketing, operations, and ultimately, the performance of the business.

Our experience shows that a three-year period, broken down into quarters, is a good horizon and cadence for planning. Twelve financial quarters is long enough to matter and short enough to plan.

Year 1				Year 2				Year 3			
Q1	Q2	Q3	Q4	Q1	Q2	Q3	Q4	Q1	Q2	Q3	Q4

- Twelve quarters
- Measurable and achievable
- Commitment creates a powerful pull on the business, demanding alignment with all of the RELAX elements
- Profit margins should be considered with revenue

Approaches to growth

There are many ways to arrive at a figure for the level of your future revenue. You want to be realistic and ambitious when choosing a revenue target. You alone will have a feel for what expansion is possible for your business based on your knowledge of customer demand, your success with marketing and advertising, the requirements and constraints on the assets you need to serve more clients and greater sales per client, your available capital to support accounts receivable and inventory, your employees' capacity, and your ability to expand the business workforce, and many more factors. It's very human to be optimistic about plans for the future. Don't be afraid to make big plans, but be careful in estimating how long it will take to get there. There's truth in the famous saying, "People consistently overestimate what they can achieve in the short term, but underestimate what they can do in the long run."

The following are only three of the many possible approaches to coming up with a revenue number:

- Top-to-bottom growth
- Steady growth assumption
- Rapid growth assumption

Top-to-bottom growth

Using your income statement, take today's total sales and declare that as your future profit. Example:

The business makes $100,000 revenue this year; and therefore, the target will be to generate $100,000 in profit in three years' time. The necessary revenue to generate that profit becomes your new top line target.

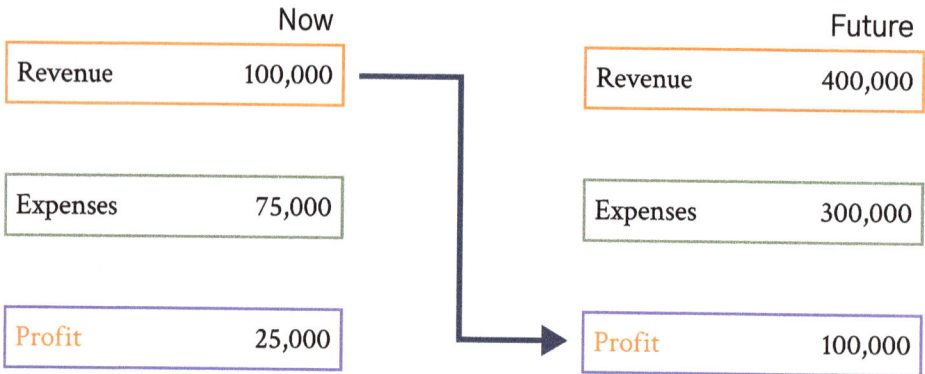

Now		Future	
Revenue	100,000	Revenue	400,000
Expenses	75,000	Expenses	300,000
Profit	25,000	Profit	100,000

Doing this requires:

- Knowing your current profit margin
- Using RELAX to calculate what revenue would generate that future profit

  In the made-up example above, the business has $100,000 in revenue and $75,000 in expenses, giving a bottom line of $25,000. This is a profit margin of 25% of revenue. For a future profit of $100,000, the future revenue will need to be $400,000, assuming the same percentage margin.

Steady growth

Steady growth will mean different things to different businesses. "Steady" suggests a consistent pace of growth, implicitly sustainable, and reliably doable for your business.

Consider picking a rate of 20%–30% increase each year, based upon all the factors such as the ones listed above in top-to-bottom growth. This is the "let's build a strong, steady business" route.

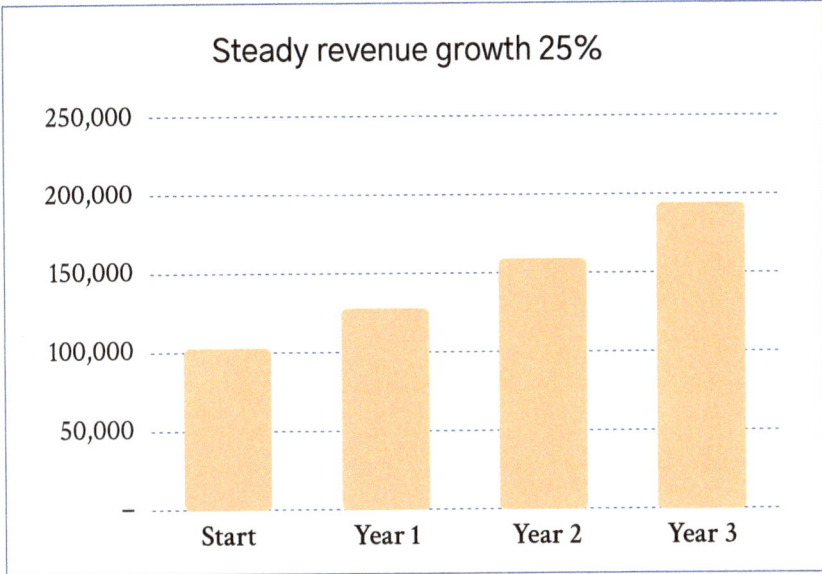

Steady revenue growth 25%

	Start	Year 1	Year 2	Year 3
250,000				
200,000				
150,000				
100,000				
50,000				

Rapid growth

Again, there's no choice that fits all business. A 30%–50% annual growth rate would make for rapid growth if you can keep it up for a few years. Perhaps you believe you can more than double your sales in two years.

A 50% annual growth rate as shown in the chart on page 88 would achieve that doubling. At that rate, the $100,000 business grows to $225,000 by the end of the second year and to nearly $350,000 by the end of the third year.

Rapid growth of 50%

400,000			
350,000			
300,000			
250,000			
200,000			
150,000			
100,000			
50,000			
	Start	Year 1	Year 2	Year 3

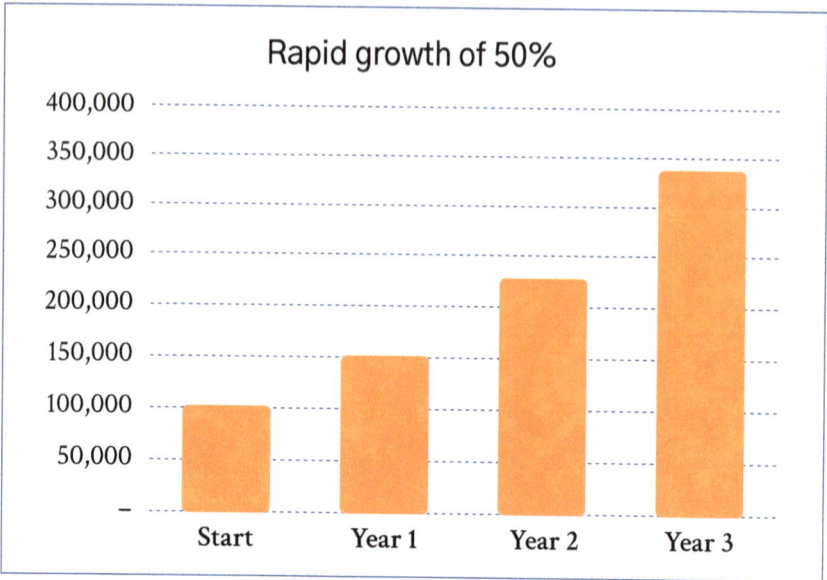

Pick an approach and a rate of growth that feels right for you. There's no perfect answer—just the one that feels true for your business, taking into account your momentum, available capacity and funding to scale up, customer demand, staff recruitment needs, etc.—all the while knowing that you will be accountable for the targets. What's most important is how this commitment to a growth target will call forth your plans and actions. Once you've committed to a three-year-out-revenue figure, you will be able to ask questions such as, "what assets will I need to get me to that revenue?" and "does my staff have capacity for this growth?" and "what sort of funding should I use to keep the wheels turning while I wait for our accounts receivable to be settled?"

CASE STUDY:

From survival to strategy

One of our workshop participants, a therapist, had been barely getting by for five years. She made enough to pay her bills but never planned beyond the next month. When challenged to declare a three-year growth target, she initially resisted: "I don't know if I'll even be in business in three years."

But something shifted when she used the RELAX framework to see her current reality:

- Revenue: $40,000/year
- Expenses: $38,000/year (mostly consisting of a modest salary for herself)
- Profit: $2,000/year (5% margin)

She decided on a steady growth model: 33% annual increase, reaching $70,000 in revenue with a 20% profit margin after two years. To achieve her goal she took these steps:

- Raised her prices by 15%
- Created a group program to leverage her time
- Invested in marketing for the first time
- Hired a virtual assistant

ACTION STEPS

- Write down your purpose in one or two sentences. Make it clear, honest, and inspiring.
- Choose a growth rate by considering a top-to-bottom objective, a steady or rapid annual growth rate, or some other growth target that feels right.
- State your three-year growth target: My revenue in three years' time ending March 31/June 30/September 30/December 31 (pick one) in _____ (fill in year) will be $_____.
- Include your profit margin: And a profit margin before tax in the third year of _____%.

What next? Bring your new business future to life

After defining your purpose and growth goals, identify misaligned systems or processes. Determine what needs to change, who to inform, and what obstacles exist. Share these commitments with your team, business partner, or a friend to solidify them.

8

RELAX system review

Now that you've stated the two critical drivers of your future value cycle—the business's purpose and revenue future—it's inevitable that this new clarity of purpose and commitment to growth will require changes to your resources and systems. So where to begin?

By now you know that the communication model and BaSIS Board with its five elements captures and describes all the finances of any business. Everything financial that happens in your business involves revenue, equity, liabilities, assets, or expenses. It's by putting those five elements to work that you have created your business's unique value cycle.

To be methodical about matching your business's resources to your stated purpose and growth rate, you can use the value cycle to guide your thinking about what's needed and what decisions you need to make.

Your future-revenue choice will make a demand on the other four elements.

By considering each element in turn, the future value cycle will become more and more real and achievable. The example considerations that follow are to give you a sense of what thinking you will bring to bear to your growth plans. You will want to involve your advisors in the detailed decision-making. Your task is to use your knowledge of the communication model and RELAX elements to engage those advisors, coaches, and employees.

Even though you may not be a financial expert, as a leader you will lead the conversations with those collaborators by asking questions and making decisions with your purpose and financial target informing your thinking.

Addressing the whole of your business

Thinking again of your business as a whole system comprising functional parts (business divisions), consider how finance touches and enables each of them: HR, marketing, sales, operations, and so on. Viewed as a wheel, **accounting and finance** sits at the center and enables every other aspect of your business.

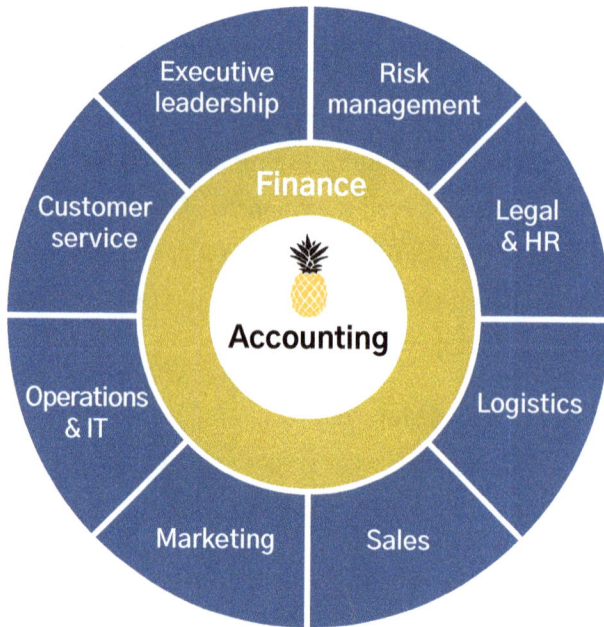

Keep in mind the parts of the systems as shown above as you explore and interrogate each of the RELAX components of the value cycle of your business. Identify and choose qualitative and quantitative changes to support your building of a future value cycle.

Various questions and considerations are listed in the examples below to get you started. Some may be relevant to your business. Others may not.

RELAX REVIEW

1. Profit review

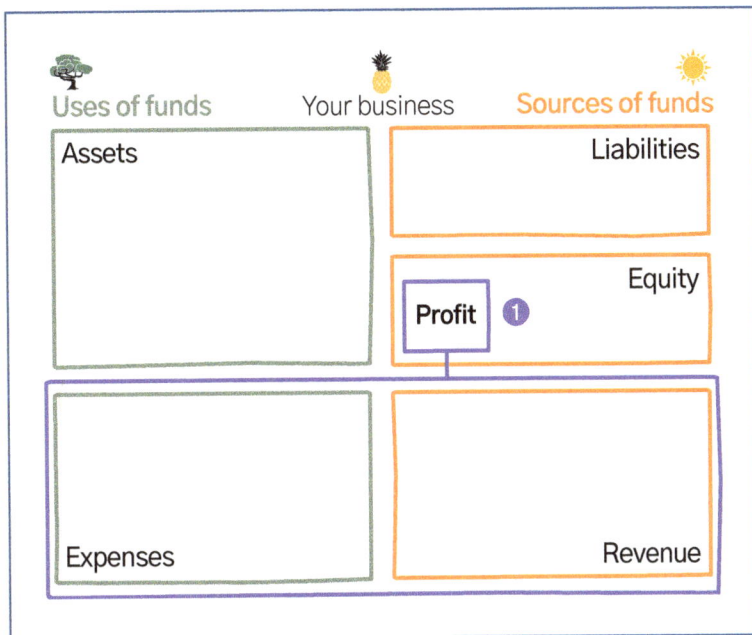

Most business owners are aiming for more profit. But not all are, and sometimes a lower profit may be deliberate, at least for a while.

There are a number of ways to achieve a higher profit:

- Increase prices
- Lower the cost of each sale
- Increase the number of sales made
- Increase the size of the business by expanding the asset base
- Lower overheads by finding efficiencies, new ways of operating, reducing premise sizes, offshoring, and/or outsourcing

Being less ambitious about your profit goals could be for reasons such as less stress, a temporary reduction to achieve long term growth, or having less money tied up in the business.

If you allow yourself a lower profit goal, use that latitude to:

- Seek revenue growth and market penetration
- Distribute cash to the owners as dividends, drawings, or increased salaries
- Maintain or increase return on equity with a reduced equity investment

2. Revenue review

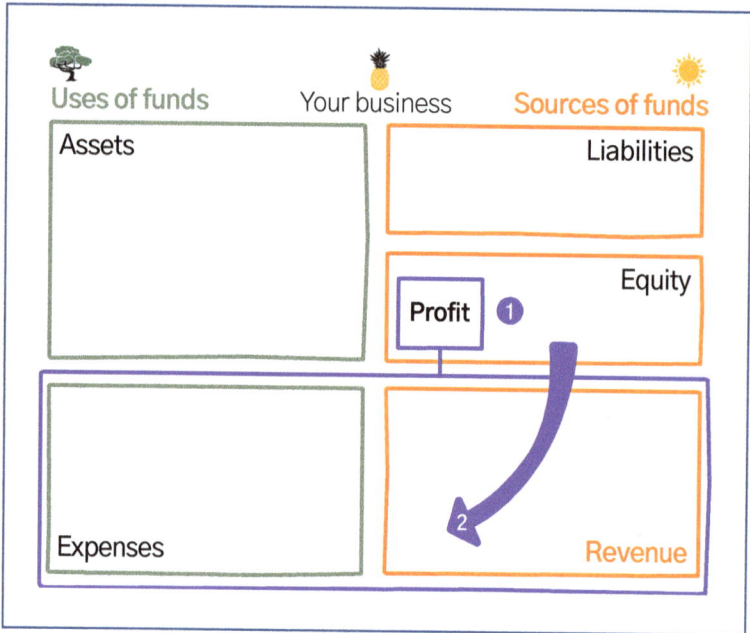

As we've seen in the previous chapters, revenue growth is a central and important focus for most business owners. But are you sure you want to run a bigger business? A smaller business might be more in line with your life goals.

Most businesses want growth, in which case consider actions such as:

- Diversifying product offering to add additional revenue streams
- Increasing prices
- Increasing volumes
- Using effective discounting to generate sales
- Diversifying markets
- Incurring more advertising and marketing expenses

- Putting a commission and incentive structure in place for anyone involved in selling (Everyone should think of themselves as involved!)

Mostly, we want more revenue, but there may be a case for wanting less:

- Consider a higher-margin lower-volume strategy by increasing prices and changing the product/service offering.
- Rightsizing: What's the right size of the business?
- Close less profitable parts of the business and eliminate some product/service offerings.
- Turn away troublesome customers.

3. Expenses review

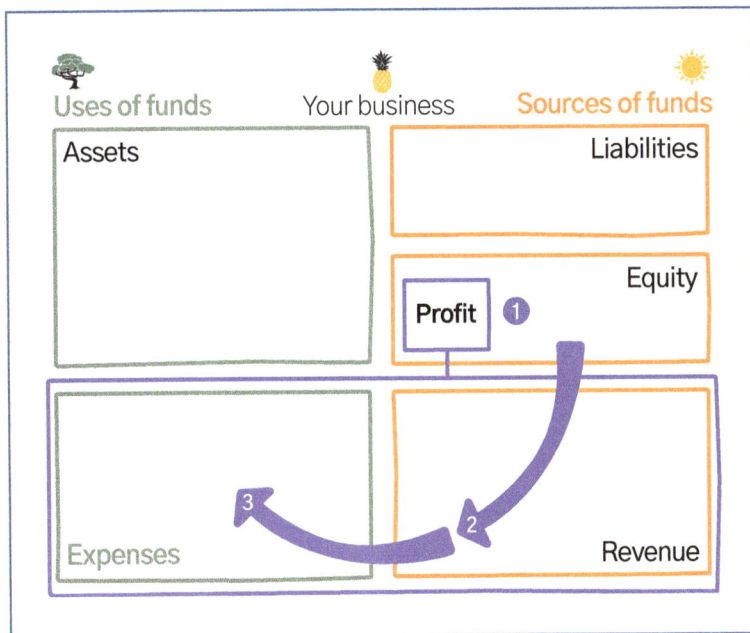

You should have mixed feelings about expenses. Reducing your expenses implies more profits given the same amount of revenue. But if you aim to increase your expenses appropriately, that increased consumption can increase your revenue by more, and therefore, increase profitability. So don't think of expenses as "bad". Rather, choose them powerfully and deliberately. For more business and profitability growth, consider:

- Are you incurring enough advertising, marketing, promotional expenses, online advertising, staff wellbeing, and staff training?
- Should you be bringing some outsourced tasks in house? Should you have a full-time or a part-time finance manager, social media manager, marketing manager? Consider insourcing versus outsourcing?
- Are you skimping on product quality, saving costs but threatening quality and reputation? Should you be increasing quality and bearing lower margins?
- Is the business paying the owner enough?
- Is all the tax due being paid?
- Does the business have enough insurance coverage? Is it taking too many risks?
- Can you incur more interest from effective borrowing? In other words, borrow more, use that money well, and incur more interest.
- Should you consider commissions and other incentives for your sales staff?

To incur less expenses, ask:

- Can you cut waste?
- Have you checked all annual and monthly subscriptions, such as software subscriptions, Zoom accounts, etc., to see if they are necessary? Can you reduce cost of goods sold to increase gross profit margins?
- Can you hire new staff in lower cost markets?
- Can you build relationship with suppliers to reduce prices in exchange for guaranteed recurring orders?
- Can you negotiate discounts?
- Can you outsource certain functions?

4. Assets review

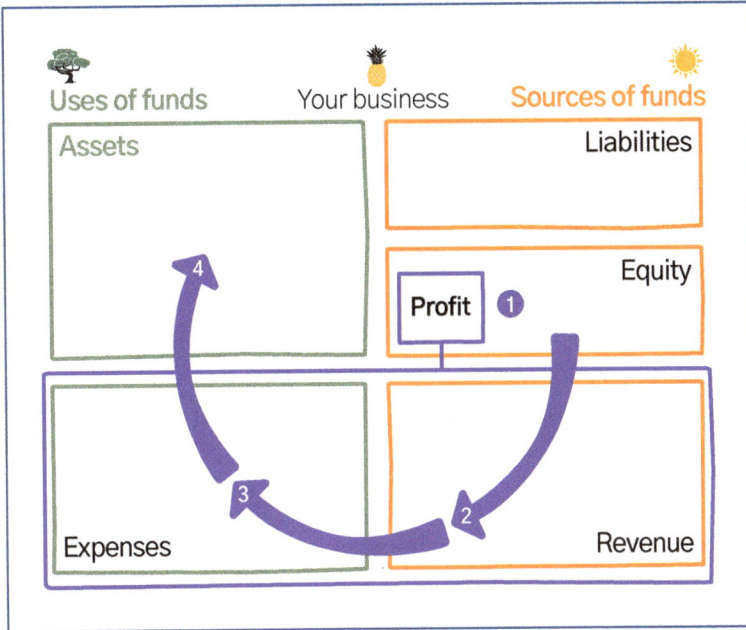

Are your current assets supporting your business goals? In order to grow the revenue and profitability of the business, it's likely that you will need to grow the asset base.

- What additional assets will the business need to enhance its capacity?
- Can you afford to offer more generous payment terms (selling more on credit and letting clients pay slowly) to attract business? This will increase the accounts receivable asset. The long-term funding of accounts receivable and inventory is called "working capital." Do you have enough working capital funding to support more accounts receivable?
- Does the business have the right mix of assets? What is the return on assets that the business is achieving? Return on assets calculates revenue per dollar of assets and profit per dollar of assets.
- Does the liquidity profile of your assets reflect the profile of your liabilities? Long-term (non-current) assets are preferably not funded with short-term liabilities.

You will at times grapple with having or needing too many assets. Give thought to considerations such as:

- Can you rent equipment instead of owning it or outsource the task altogether? (For example, Apple doesn't manufacture its iPhones, so it doesn't own factories.)
- Can you offload non-productive assets?
- Do you have too much cash? Are you too cautious about distributing cash to owners?
- Are your receivables turning into cash fast enough? Can you reduce the accounts receivable balance by collecting payment from customers sooner?

5. Liabilities review

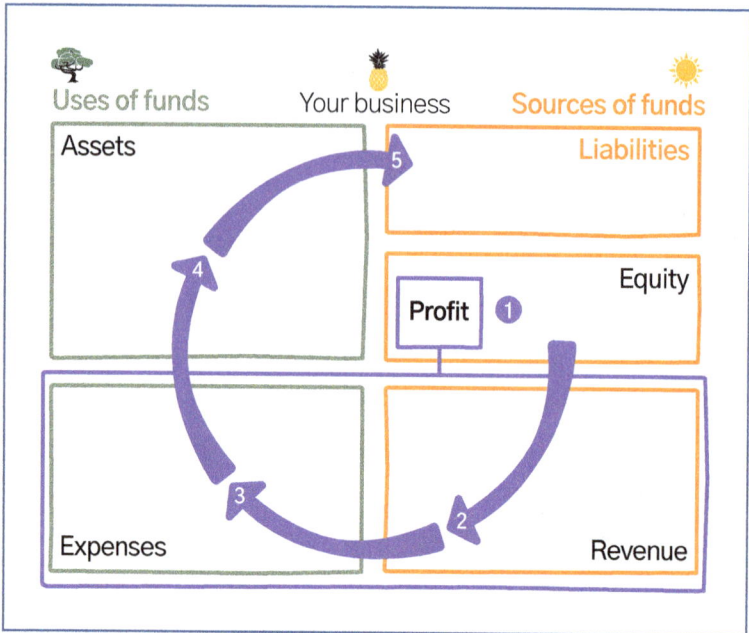

Are you using debt wisely? Could more and better financing options help you scale?

Consider what an expansion of the business's non-equity funding might achieve:

- Should the business increase total liabilities through new borrowing? What could it do with more borrowed cash?
- Can the business afford to service additional debt? Will it make enough

profit to cover interest?

- Would the business benefit from more of a particular kind of debt, like a lower-interest bank loan to replace high-interest credit card debt?
- Can the business get liability funding by sourcing up-front payments from customers as "deferred revenue" liabilities?
- Can the business get longer payment terms with suppliers thus increasing accounts payable?

Consider also how the business might reduce its debt burden:

- Can the business save interest by paying down liabilities?
- Is the business sitting on too much idle cash? Should it pay off loans with that cash?
- Can the business convert some debt to equity? This will dilute existing shareholders.
- Should the business sell some assets to repay debt?
- Can the business consolidate debt under one lender with better terms?

6. Share capital review

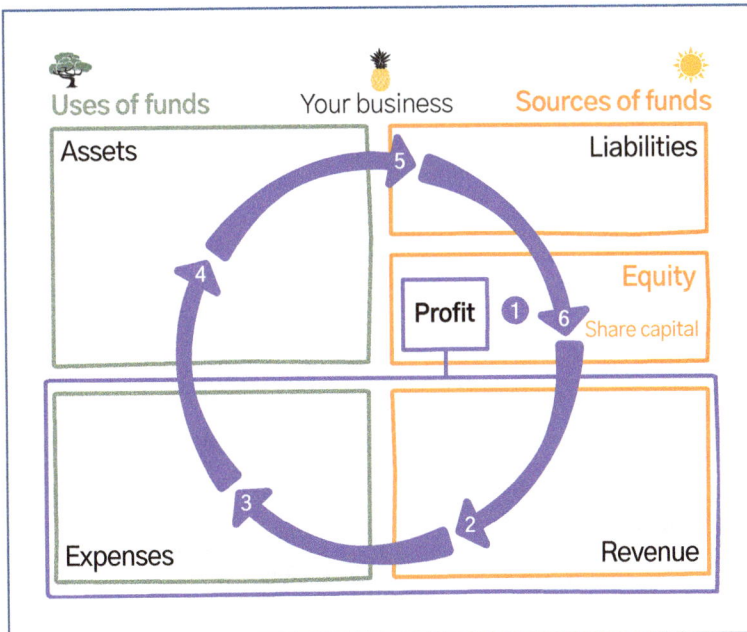

Are you investing in your business strategically? Could outside investors support your growth? If more equity share capital is needed:

- What would the business do with a fresh injection of cash from equity?
- Would that investment come from current co-owners, or new owners?
- If new owners, would they be active or silent shareholders?
- Who has control of the business through majority votes to select the board?
- Would more equity unleash greater ability to borrow?
- Does borrowing from shareholders make more sense than investment as equity?

If less equity share capital is required:

- Should the business buy out some shareholders?
- Is a management buyout something to consider, replacing non-involved owners?
- Does the business want to increase "return on equity" by using less equity to make the same level of profit?

FOLLOW UP ACTION STEPS

Pick out a few of the RELAX value cycle considerations above that you feel are pertinent to your business. Share them with your finance or operations team and discuss them at a monthly or quarterly finance and performance review meeting.

TESTIMONIAL

> **"**
> Since we've started this class I look at daily things that I do differently. I catch myself either thinking more about "Could we be generating more income if we were doing this a little differently?" Before I was focused on just the day-to-day, and I realized I needed an assistant and hired someone to help me get through the routine challenges. Now I'm able to look a little further out and see what we can really do to start making a difference to the bottom line. - Kristine R., Deputy Director

9

Empowering your foundation for financial success

As you reach the final chapters of this journey, it's time to reflect on the powerful financial skills and mindset shifts you've gained and how they come together to empower you as a business owner and leader.

What you've learned about your business's finances

Throughout this book, you've discovered that your business's financial reports— the income statement and balance sheet—are not just numbers on a page. They are a language, a communication model, that tells the story of your business's health, value, and potential.

- **The balance sheet butterfly:** You've seen how the balance sheet shows a snapshot of your business's assets and the promises made to funders— owners, lenders, and customers. This dual perspective helps you understand where your business stands at any moment and how it's financed.

- **The income statement and BaSIS Board:** You've learned that the income statement reveals how your business creates and consumes value over time through value-generating activities and value-sacrificing activities. The BaSIS Board ties these elements together, showing how profit grows equity and how every transaction impacts your business's financial position.

- **RELAX framework:** The five elements—Revenue, Equity, Liabilities, Assets, and eXpenses—form a complete communication model. Understanding these allows you to "read" your business's financial story clearly and confidently.
- **Value cycle:** You discovered how the RELAX parts of your business interact to form a living cycle that represents your business at work to achieve its purpose.
- *Pow-pow* **thinking:** You now appreciate that every business event has two impacts, maintaining balance and telling a full story. This mindset helps you see beyond cash flow to the real value movements in your business.
- **Future value cycle:** You have gotten clearer on your business's purpose and chosen a financial revenue target. Together, these work together to establish a future value cycle.

What does this have to do with your financial decision making?

With these tools, you're no longer guessing or overwhelmed by financial reports. Instead, you can:

- **Make objective decisions:** By separating yourself from your business and working inside the business communication model and its five elements, you see the facts clearly. You can evaluate opportunities and risks based on what's best for the business, not just what feels comfortable or familiar.
- **Plan your future:** Using your income statement and balance sheet as maps, and with your understanding of the business's value cycle, you can set realistic growth targets, budget effectively, and allocate resources wisely. You understand how revenue growth, expense control, and asset management work together to build equity and long-term value.
- **Spot opportunities and challenges early:** You can identify cash flow issues, leverage debt strategically, and recognize hidden assets. This foresight helps you steer your business proactively rather than reactively.
- **Communicate with confidence:** Whether talking with your operations team, your advisors and coach, your bookkeeper, or your bank, you now speak the language of business finance. This clarity builds trust and opens doors to partnerships and support.

The role of accountability in your leadership

All these skills and insights rest on one essential foundation: Accountability.

Accountability involves honoring commitments to yourself, your business, team, and customers; being honest about financial reports; following through; and creating reliable systems. Without being accountable, even the best financial plans fall apart. When you build a business that's whole, trustworthy, and resilient, your financial systems become a source of strength, not stress.

You've discovered the power of separating yourself from your business—the pineapple concept—and how that shift opens doors to new possibilities. You've learned to speak the language of business and finance, to see your business as a living system of value, and to envision a future that excites you.

Without accountability, the system falters. Plans become empty words. Growth stalls. Trust erodes. When you build a culture where people know what to expect and can rely on each other, you create momentum that carries you through challenges and propels you toward your new business future.

You may be wondering what that might look like for you. Below are a few practices we have put in place in our own organizations.

Kelly has established a system where her bookkeeper shares Leaders Team's monthly income statement and balance sheet by the tenth of the month. Kelly reviews and has the information available when making financial decisions throughout the month.

In addition, Kelly receives a weekly cash flow report so that she can see what inflows and outflows are coming up. She's diligent about putting aside 25% of cash flow from revenue into a savings account to cover taxes and other fees.

At Leaders Team's weekly team meeting, each coach's scoreboard is reviewed to track individual team members' performance. The weekly meeting begins with team members reading the company's purpose to ensure that the team is operating and aligned with it.

Peter meets with his team each Wednesday to review all of Wealthvox's projects, which are tracked on a shared spreadsheet/workbook accessible to the whole team.

The first tab of the workbook states the company's mission. The next tab in the workbook lists the projects, and each project is then described on its own tabbed spreadsheet where the people who are accountable for the project are listed with deadlines.

For financial management specifically, Peter receives financial statements from his bookkeeper/financial manager monthly and then reviews them at a scheduled meeting with his part-time CFO and another director.

A cash flow forecast is updated weekly, and the finance manager alerts the relevant team members if there are any upcoming issues with receipt delays and imminent payment obligations.

What practices will you put in place?

- Are your financial systems working? What do you need to put in place and who do you need to involve?
- How will you keep track of people's performance?
- How will you regularly align your team with the business purpose?
- How will your business live up to its promises to you, your team, your customers, and your community?

The power of internal and external team alignment

YOU DON'T HAVE TO DO THIS ALONE.

Your business is a system made up of people, processes, and purpose. Aligning your internal team around your financial goals and business purpose creates clarity and momentum.

Equally important is your external expert team—your coach, bookkeeper, attorney, marketing professional, and others. You don't need to be *the* expert in every area. What matters is having trusted experts you can rely on and talk with confidently. Together, your aligned internal and external teams become a powerful force that supports your leadership, amplifies your strengths, and helps your business thrive.

You are not your business – you are the leader of its future

Remember, you are not your business. You are the leader, the visionary, the steward of a living system.

Your business has its own life and energy. When you step back and see yourself as part of this bigger system—working within the language of business, being accountable, and aligned with your team—you gain freedom and power.

You're no longer limited by old personal beliefs or personal doubts. You're free to design and implement a purpose for your business that excites you.

What's next? Your invitation to lead with confidence

The tools, frameworks, and mindset shifts are in your hands.

Now it's time to:

- Honor your commitments and build trust.
- Use your financial skills to make clear, confident decisions that grow your business.
- Build and nurture a team—internal and external—that shares your vision and values.
- Embrace your role as a leader of a system, not just a solo operator.
- Celebrate the freedom and power that comes from knowing you are part of something bigger.

Your future—and the future of your business—is bright, full of possibility, and waiting for you to step into it.

Take a deep breath, smile, and get ready. Your new story is just beginning.

Kelly video

How to achieve breakthrough results

The transformation you've experienced reading this book is only the foundation. The real work happens when you apply these tools consistently in your business.

What other business leaders are saying about our work

"It was an excellent training. I really think this training should be mandatory for business owners."

– Tiffany S., Small Business Owner

"This is invaluable to entrepreneurs starting their own businesses. It is a foundation that is a must."

– Christine H., Workshop Participant

Ready to go deeper?

The business owners who achieve breakthrough results don't stop with knowledge. They invest in ongoing support and accountability; they recognize that sustainable transformation requires:

- **Consistent application** of these frameworks in real business situations
- **Ongoing guidance** as they encounter new challenges

- **Community connection** with other leaders on similar journeys
- **Accountability structures** that ensure declarations become reality

That's where we can help. Leaders Team specializes in cracking the code for high-performance and breakthrough results. Our skilled transformational coaches can guide you and your team to unlock the true power of your organization and help you achieve unprecedented results.

As a reader of this book, we invite you to visit **www.PineappleandProfits.com** to schedule a complimentary business strategy consultation to explore how these concepts apply specifically to you and your business. Whether you're struggling with cash flow, planning for growth, or building your team's financial literacy, we'll help you create a customized roadmap.

We offer:

- One-on-one executive coaching
- Custom corporate coaching
- Small business coaching for businesses of all sizes
- Workshops for "Investing in Your Future," "The Foundation of Transformational Leadership," "Being a Leader," "Reinventing the Future," and many more for you and your team members.

Visit us at **www.PineappleandProfits.com** to learn more about our work and for detailed course descriptions.

The question isn't whether you're capable of transformation—you've already begun. The question is, "How quickly do you want to accelerate your progress?"

Your business deserves a leader who operates with financial clarity, personal integrity, and unwavering commitment to the declared future. That leader is you.

● ● ●

ᵾᴡealthvox

Wealthvox is a global education company dedicated to making financial literacy and business acumen accessible, clear, and engaging. Since 1998, Peter Frampton and the Wealthvox team have developed the Color Accounting learning method, an innovative methodology that uses simple visual frameworks to teach accounting and finance concepts in a way anyone can understand.

Wealthvox works with educators, companies, and professional bodies worldwide to build financial capability and confidence, and holds all intellectual property rights in the Color Accounting learning method.

For more information, visit wealthvox.com.

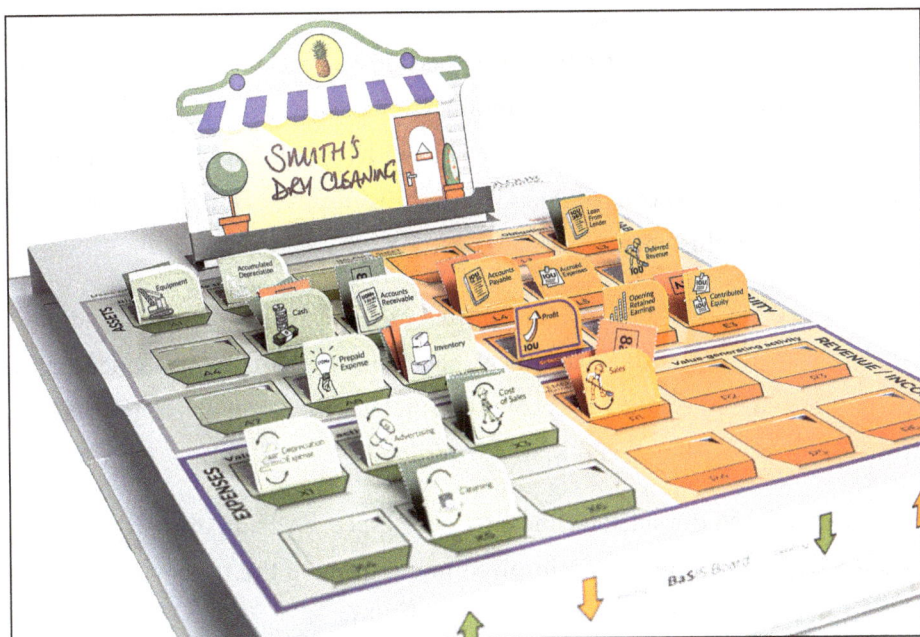

● ● ●

Acknowledgments

There are so many people I could acknowledge for their unique contributions, but I will focus on those directly related to this book.

First and foremost, I acknowledge Rich Townsend for opening the door to the world of transformation and what it can offer a lifetime and career. I have had amazing mentors in transformational thinking: Werner Erhard and many of his champions and colleagues, including Molly Partridge, Julia Whitaker, and Diane and Joe DiMaggio.

I appreciate the partnerships that made this book possible with Peter Frampton, and Gina Donato, and the C2 Communications team. I would never have met Peter if not for my joint venture relationship with Brian Lanier and Jon Ouellette. And thank you, to Robyn Perlman and the BLI team who inspired the workshops that led to this book.

I have great appreciation for my professional team, who directly support Leaders Team—Jeanne Seewald and Michele Johnson; for our strategic alliance partner, Debbie King; and for my colleagues at Leaders Team—Diane DiMaggio, Kim Wynn, Jody daSilva, and Mariel Juanillo.

I'm grateful for all the small business owners, especially from my community of women business owners, who inspired me to develop the programs and consulting engagements that have been truly fulfilling.

My partnership with Peter Frampton has been an awesome experience, and I look forward to more endeavors with the Wealthvox team. Peter brings joy to the world of accounting and helped open the door for Leaders Team to build a scalable business, which we are currently developing with the team from Get Scalable, who continue to educate and inspire our team's potential.

Finally, I'm grateful for my daughter, Rikki, and my friend, Sharon Hood, as my sounding boards and creativity partners.

This book represents just the beginning of what Peter and I offer to our clients, and we look forward to meeting you.

– Kelly Townsend

I chose to co-author this book because of Kelly—who she is and what she stands for. Kelly, I continue to learn from you every time we work together and am enormously grateful for our friendship and collaboration. Thank you, to you and your team.

I also want to acknowledge my colleagues at Wealthvox who make this work and collaboration possible every day. They enable us to move forward step-by-step, toward the world we see where everyone has access to the financial conversations in life. Conversations in which fear and limitation are overcome and prosperity and freedom bloom. Karien, thank you especially for your work and talents infused into the book.

– Peter Frampton

About the authors

Kelly Townsend

Kelly Townsend is the principal for Leaders Team and has a thirty-five-year history working with both large enterprises and small- to medium-sized businesses. This experience provides her with a deep understanding of the challenges faced by her clients. For the past twenty years, she has developed breakthrough results for organizations, transformed leadership skills and aligned teams in a range of sectors globally including healthcare, construction, legal, and financial services.

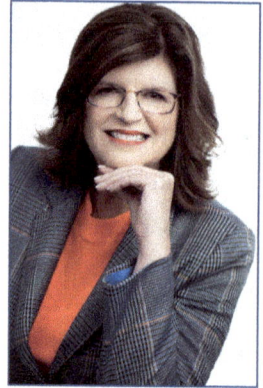

Kelly's passion and rare ability to listen and hear what is happening at a deeper level with her clients—and understand what is missing—sets her apart from other transformational management consultants. She is on a mission to create transformation and possibility for each and every one of them.

Leaders Team clients go on to become the kind of leaders who are needed in the world today.

Kelly is based in Naples, Florida.

Peter Frampton

Peter Frampton is the CEO of Wealthvox, a financial education organization that enables people to have better financial conversations.

Peter graduated from the University of Cape Town and founded South Africa's oldest tech incubator that helped generate several technology ecosystems, including edtech, fintech, and biotech communities. He qualified as a Chartered Accountant at KPMG Australia.

He recently won the Middlesex University (UK) medal for his contribution to financial inclusion. He has taught at many businesses and universities and is on the adjunct faculty of American University in Washington, DC.

Peter lives in Geneva, Switzerland.

Templates and resources

Pause and reflect:

Where might you be collapsing yourself and your business?

Accounting is a language.

Enjoy our one-page reference to support thinking in the model.

Draw your own Butterfly Balance Sheet.

Practice seeing double.

Use this quick decision-check using the RELAX model.

Clarify the purpose of your business.

If this way of seeing resonates, stay connected.

Glossary of terms

Accountability	The fact or condition of being accountable; required or expected to justify actions or decisions. As a verb, consider or regard in a specified way; make favorable or unfavorable expression of performance.
Accounting	Derives from the word "count." So does the word "accountable." Accounting enables accountability. To be accountable is to be responsible for something. Having the power to respond. "Response-able." It is about tracking what's happening with money. At its simplest, accounting is a system of sorting and grouping information about resources.
Accounting duality	The accounting duality is the context in which a business's assets are tracked, as well as the funding of the assets with obligations. This double-tracking is what makes accounting more than an asset register. It tracks the accountability for the assets. The accounting duality represents sources of funds (energy) and uses of funds (energy).
Assets	Anything valuable is an asset. Being valuable is the unique quality of assets. They're recorded on the "uses" side of the balance sheet.

Recognized assets: Shown on the balance sheet.

Unrecognized assets: Not shown on the balance sheet for reasons such as being not reliably measurable or because the assets aren't exclusively under the business's control.

Classifying assets: Assets divide into several categories:

Cash: Cash in the bank or on-hand is an asset that takes up a lot of management's time, making sure there's enough of it and managing the timing and rate of cash flowing into and out of the business.

Tangible assets: Physical items such as buildings, equipment, and furniture.

Intangible assets: Non-physical assets like patents, trademarks, and brand reputation.

Recognized assets: Items formally recorded on the balance sheet, such as cash, inventory, and those mentioned above.

Unrecognized assets: Valuable elements not captured in financial statements, like customer loyalty or company culture.

Other categories of assets: Other intangible assets that might appear on a balance sheet.

Deposits: If you have paid a deposit on a lease, for example, that deposit recorded on the balance sheet is an asset because it represents your right to get your deposit money back.

Accounts receivable: This is the right to be paid. It's not money, but represents the current right to collect money in the future.

Intellectual property: Intellectual property can take the form of, for example, secret ways of manufacturing your products, templates, operating manuals, patents, copyrights, and logos.

Measuring assets: There is no singular truth about the value of an asset. There's no one true number. Valuation is subjective. Assets can be measured in different ways, including:

Historical cost: The price paid for an asset.

Market value: The price at which an asset could be sold on an active market.

Fair value: The amount for which two reasonable people would agree to exchange the asset.

Replacement cost: The cost to replace the asset with a similar one.

Present value: The current worth of future cash flows; the present right to receive cash in the future.

Realizable value: The amount that the seller could get for the asset under the circumstances, which might be a liquidation event where "everything must go," and which amount could be reduced by an agent's commission. The amount might be less than the normal market value.

Balance sheet	The central financial report that tells us "what's so"—the truth about any business. The balance sheet tells us what assets the business was using at a particular moment and how it financed those assets. Also called the Statement of Position, the balance sheet shows what the business has and what promises it made. It shows the sources of business energy and the uses of the business energy.
Balance sheet vs. income statement	The balance sheet represents where a business is "at"—a snapshot in time. The income statement tells the story of how it got there and how it's doing in terms of generating and sacrificing value.
BaSIS Board™	The heart of our framework. It's a way to shift how you relate to your business. When you can name each of the RELAX elements, locate them on your financial reports, and understand how they interact, you begin to see your business as an integrated system. Not just a collection of transactions, but a living cycle of value creation.

The name comes from **Ba**lance **S**heet plus **I**ncome **S**tatement. The top three boxes are the balance sheet, the same butterfly we've been using. And the bottom two boxes form the income statement, which now explains how the profit in the equity section was generated.

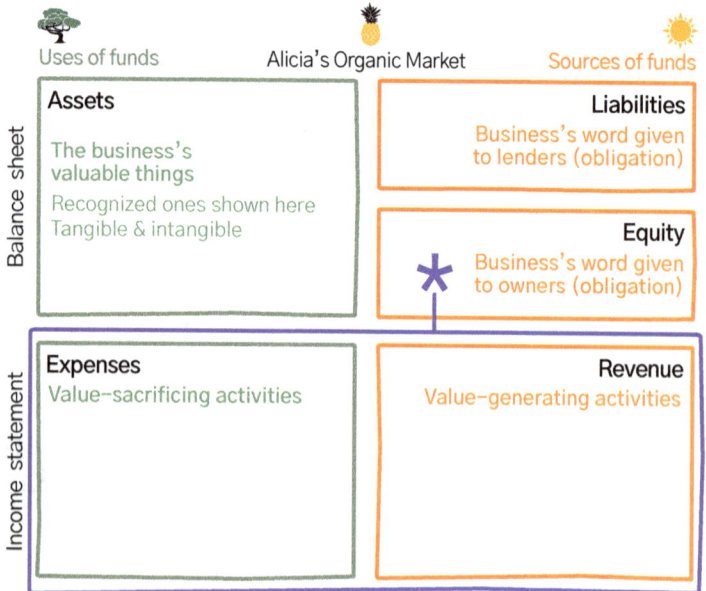

Uses of funds	Alicia's Organic Market	Sources of funds
Assets		**Liabilities**
The business's valuable things		Business's word given to lenders (obligation)
Recognized ones shown here Tangible & intangible		**Equity**
		Business's word given to owners (obligation)
Expenses		**Revenue**
Value–sacrificing activities		Value–generating activities

Balance sheet

Income statement

Business acumen   The know-how to operate effectively in business.

Butterfly metaphor   The butterfly diagram is a representation of the balance sheet to high-light the duality. The orange, right-hand wing of the butterfly shows how the business sourced its assets: by incurring promises to funders, which promises energized the business. The green, left-hand side of the butterfly shows the assets that were funded with the energy.

Chart of accounts   The list of groupings used to track business activities and assets. The chart reflects the five top-level RELAX groups. Subcategories are chosen to provide the level of detail the users need.

Color Accounting™   The Color Accounting learning method is an educational system developed by Wealthvox. It uses the BaSIS Board as a communication framework to illustrate the finances of your business in a single diagram.

Color Accounting uses **orange** to represent sources of funds and **green** to represent uses of funds. This aligns with the orthodox concept of debits and credits. Debits are green; credits are orange.

Obligations and revenue are credit accounts. They energize the business, like orange sunshine.

Assets and expenses are debit accounts. They are like the green garden that the energy feeds.

Communication model   The set of words, ideas, and rules we use to talk about something. In this book, it is the conversation or the financial story of your business. When you look at an income statement or balance sheet, consider that you're looking at a communication model that makes up a world that allows you to see your business in a new way.

Equity   The business's promises to its owners.

Expenses   Activity that decreases profit by consuming assets (or causes an increase in liabilities). Value-sacrificing activity.

Finance   Finance is the marshalling and use of a business's energy, described and measured by accounting. Making promises and doing work are sources of energy. Acquiring and holding assets and consuming resources are uses of energy. Money is one very important store of energy.

Income statement	Describes performance and activities. The income statement is referred to by many names, including profit and loss statement, P&L, statement of financial performance, statement of operations, and statement of activities. This reminds us that it describes performance and activities.
Leverage	A way to amplify the business's financial capacity by using debt to pursue growth and profitability beyond what owner-provided funding alone would allow.
Liabilities	The business's promises to lenders or creditors.
Pineapple	Represents the collapse in your personal identity with your business and the limiting beliefs you then bring to these collapsed contexts.
"Pow-pow" thinking	The practice of "thinking double." It's a reminder that whenever anything happens in your business—when a financial transaction takes place—the financial communication framework is impacted twice.
Profit	On the balance sheet, profit is a type of equity. It is the part of the obligation to the owner that came about due to the activities of the business. The generated obligation to owners. Profit contrasts with contributed equity, which is the promise to the owner that resulted from the owner putting assets into the business. Profit is not an asset. Profit also appears on the income statement to show the net value generation that the business performed. This is calculated as value-generating activity less value-sacrificing activity.
RELAX	RELAX is the mnemonic for the five fundamental elements that make up the accounting system. They are **R**evenue, **E**quity, **L**iabilities, **A**ssets, and e**X**penses. Assets, liabilities, and equity appear on the balance sheet. Revenue and expenses appear on the income statement.
Revenue	Activity that increases profit by increasing assets (or decreasing liabilities). Value-generating activity.
Sources of funds and uses of funds	Revenue, equity, and liabilities are sources of energy. Assets and expenses are the uses of energy.

Team alignment An aligned internal and external team becomes a powerful force that supports your leadership, amplifies your strengths, and helps your business thrive.

> *Internal alignment:* Aligning your internal team around your financial goals and business purpose creates clarity and momentum.

> *External alignment.* Having trusted experts you can rely on and converse with confidently.

Three key dimensions to understand accounting *Language:* The special words used in accounting. Language refers to the words and what they specifically mean in the context of the domain and accounting duality. Many specialized terms make up the world of accounting. You've likely heard many of these terms before, but they are often poorly explained and widely misunderstood because in casual conversation people use them in a non-dualistic way. Clear financial communication requires terms to be used with an appreciation of the duality. For example, revenue and cash are two different things in the duality.

Structure: How financial reports (like balance sheets and income statements) are set up. This dimension focuses on how financial information and reports are organized. For example, why does a balance sheet have two sides? How does the income statement connect to and fit into the balance sheet?

Logic: Understanding how account-totals increase or decrease when the business transacts and how the balance sheet always stays in balance. When something happens in your business, the sides of the butterfly must both increase, decrease, or stay the same, because the impacts of the transaction cancel each other out on the same butterfly wing.

Value cycle The value cycle shows how the five elements work together to achieve the business's purpose. When you appreciate the dance of the elements, you'll begin to see your business not just as a stream of numbers but as a living, evolving system of value exchange.

Value cycle narrative How you give voice to the story of your business. The five RELAX elements of the communication model form the basis of the bigger picture narrative that includes your income statement and your balance sheet. The value cycle narrative captures the purpose and operating method of the business.

Profit maximization purpose: Elements of the business interact with the intention of growing its promise to its owners.

Social impact: Elements of the business interact with the intention of creating change external to the business to make an impact on a chosen community.

Planning and budgeting: The business plans the interaction of the future elements of the business to achieve its goals and create a future value cycle.

Wheel of business   In this visual representation of your business, each spoke stands for a part of your business and the center of the wheel, accounting and finance, connects the parts.

Attributions

The presentation of the accounting and financial content in this book is based upon the Color Accounting™ learning method, developed since 1998 and exclusively owned by Wealthvox Innovation Limited. Wealthvox gratefully acknowledges the contributions of its global community of educators in developing and advancing this learning system.

Some of the ideas in this book are based on the work of Werner Erhard and Landmark Worldwide and their course "Being a Leader and the Effective Exercise of Leadership: An Ontological/Phenomenological Model," authored by Werner Erhard, Michael C. Jensen, and Steve Zaffron and © Copyright 2014, W. Erhard, M. Jensen, Landmark Worldwide LLC and are used with permission.

www.ingramcontent.com/pod-product-compliance
Lightning Source LLC
Chambersburg PA
CBHW071429210326
41597CB00020B/3708